Bernie Sanders Revolution

Title: Bernie Sanders Revolution

ISBN-13: 978-1-942825-32-6

Author: Kambiz Mostofizadeh

Publisher: Mikazuki Publishing House

Description: This book explores the ideas of Vermont Senator Bernie Sanders and his political movement to change America.

I0039128

Bernie Sanders Revolution

June 14. 2016 Bernie Sanders Speech
Election days come and go. But political and social revolutions that attempt to transform our society never end. They continue every day, every week and every month in the fight to create a nation of social and economic justice. That's what the trade union movement is about. That's what the civil rights movement is about. That's what the women's movement is about. That's what the gay rights movement is about. That's what the environmental movement is about. And that's what this campaign has been about over the past year. That's what the political revolution is about and that's why the political revolution must continue into the future. Real change never takes place from the top down, or in the living rooms of wealthy campaign contributors. It always occurs from the bottom on up when tens of millions of people say "enough is enough" and become engaged in the fight for justice. That's what the political

Bernie Sanders Revolution

revolution we helped start is all about. That's
why the political revolution must continue.
When we began this campaign a little over a
year ago, we had no political organization, no
money and very little name recognition. The
media determined that we were a fringe
campaign. Nobody thought we were going
anywhere. Well, a lot has changed over a year.
During this campaign, we won more than 12
million votes. We won 22 state primaries and
caucuses. We came very close – within 2 points
or less in five more states. In other words, our
vision for the future of this country is not some
kind of fringe idea. It is not a radical idea. It is
mainstream. It is what millions of Americans
believe in and want to see happen.
And something else extraordinarily important
happened in this campaign that makes me very
optimistic about the future of our country
something that, frankly, I had not anticipated. In
virtually every state that we contested we won

Bernie Sanders Revolution

the overwhelming majority of the votes of people 45 years of age or younger, sometimes, may I say, by huge numbers. These are the people who are determined to shape the future of this country. These are the people who are the future of this country. Together, in this campaign, 1.5 million people came out to our rallies and town meetings in almost every state in the country. Together, hundreds of thousands of volunteers made 75 million phone calls urging their fellow citizens into action. Together, our canvassers knocked on more than 5 million doors. Together, we hosted 74,000 meetings in every state and territory in this country. Together, 2.7 million people made over 8 million individual contributions to our campaign more contributions at this point than any campaign in American history. Amazingly, the bulk of those contributions came from low-income and working people whose donations averaged $27 apiece. In an unprecedented way, we showed

Bernie Sanders Revolution

the world that we could run a strong national campaign without being dependent on the big-money interests whose greed has done so much to damage our country. And let me give a special thanks to the financial support we received from students struggling to repay their college loans, from seniors and disabled vets on Social Security, from workers earning starvation wages and even from people who were unemployed. In every single state that we contested we took on virtually the entire political establishment U.S. senators, members of Congress, governors, mayors, state legislators and local party leaders. To those relatively few elected officials who had the courage to stand with us, I say thank you. We must continue working together into the future. This campaign has never been about any single candidate. It is always about transforming America. It is about ending a campaign finance system which is corrupt and allows billionaires to buy elections.

Bernie Sanders Revolution

It is about ending the grotesque level of wealth and income inequality that we are experiencing where almost all new wealth and income goes to the people on top, where the 20 wealthiest people own more wealth than the bottom 150 million. It is about creating an economy that works for all of us, not just the 1 percent.

It is about ending the disgrace of native Americans who live on the Pine Ridge, South Dakota, reservation having a life expectancy lower than many third-world countries.

It is about ending the incredible despair that exists in many parts of this country where as a result of unemployment and low wages, suicide, drugs and alcohol millions of Americans are now dying, in an ahistorical way, at a younger age than their parents. It is about ending the disgrace of having the highest level of childhood poverty of almost any major country on earth and having public school systems in inner cities that are totally failing our children where kids

Bernie Sanders Revolution

now stand a greater chance of ending up in jail than ending up with a college degree. It is about ending the disgrace that millions of undocumented people in this country continue to live in fear and are exploited every day on their jobs because they have no legal rights. It is about ending the disgrace of tens of thousands of Americans dying every year from preventable deaths because they either lack health insurance, have high deductibles or cannot afford the outrageously high cost of the prescription drugs they need. It is about ending the disgrace of hundreds of thousands of bright young people unable to go to college because their families are poor or working class, while millions more struggle with suffocating levels of student debt. It is about ending the pain of a young single mother in Nevada, in tears, telling me that she doesn't know how she and her daughter can make it on $10.45 an hour. And

Bernie Sanders Revolution

the reality that today millions of our fellow
Americans are working at starvation wages.
It is about ending the disgrace of a mother in
Flynt, Michigan, telling me what has happened
to the intellectual development of her child as a
result of lead in the water in that city, of many
thousands of homes in California and other
communities unable to drink the polluted water
that comes out of their faucets. In America. In
the year 2016. In a nation whose infrastructure
is crumbling before our eyes. It is about ending
the disgrace that too many veterans still sleep
out on the streets, that homelessness is
increasing and that tens of millions of
Americans, because of a lack of affordable
housing, are paying 40, 50 percent or more of
their limited incomes to put a roof over their
heads. It is about ending the disgrace that, in a
given year, corporations making billions in profit
avoid paying a nickel in taxes because they
stash their money in the Cayman Islands and

other tax havens. This campaign is about
defeating Donald Trump, the Republican
candidate for president. After centuries of
racism, sexism and discrimination of all forms in
our country we do not need a major party
candidate who makes bigotry the cornerstone of
his campaign. We cannot have a president who
insults Mexicans and Latinos, Muslims, women
and African-Americans. We cannot have a
president who, in the midst of so much income
and wealth inequality, wants to give hundreds of
billions of dollars in tax breaks to the very rich.
We cannot have a president who, despite all of
the scientific evidence, believes that climate
change is a hoax. The major political task that
we face in the next five months is to make
certain that Donald Trump is defeated and
defeated badly. And I personally intend to begin
my role in that process in a very short period of
time. But defeating Donald Trump cannot be our
only goal. We must continue our grassroots

...ate the America that we know we

. become. And we must take that energy into the Democratic National Convention on July 25 in Philadelphia where we will have more than 1,900 delegates. I recently had the opportunity to meet with Secretary Clinton and discuss some of the very important issues facing our country and the Democratic Party. It is no secret that Secretary Clinton and I have strong disagreements on some very important issues. It is also true that our views are quite close on others. I look forward, in the coming weeks, to continued discussions between the two campaigns to make certain that your voices are heard and that the Democratic Party passes the most progressive platform in its history and that Democrats actually fight for that agenda. I also look forward to working with Secretary Clinton to transform the Democratic Party so that it becomes a party of working people and young people, and not just wealthy campaign contributors: a party that has the courage to take on Wall Street, the pharmaceutical industry, the fossil fuel industry and the other powerful special interests that dominate our political and economic life. As I have said throughout this campaign, the Democratic Party must support raising the federal minimum wage to $15 an hour, and create millions of jobs rebuilding our crumbling infrastructure.

We must ensure that women will no longer make 79-cents on the dollar compared to men and that we fight for pay equity. We must fight to make certain that women throughout the country have the right to control their own bodies.

We must protect the right of our gay brothers and sisters to marriage equality in every state America. As the recent tragedy in Orlando has made crystal clear, we must ban the sale and distribution of assault weapons, end the gun show loophole and expand instant background checks. We must defeat the Trans-Pacific

...p and make certain that that bad trade ...r does not get a vote in a lame-duck session of Congress. We must resist all efforts to cut Social Security and, in fact, expand benefits for our seniors and disabled veterans. We must understand that the greed, recklessness and illegal behavior on Wall Street has to end, that we need to pass modern-day Glass-Steagall legislation and that we need to break up the biggest financial institutions in this country who not only remain too big to fail but who prevent the kind of vigorous competition that a healthy financial system requires. We must aggressively combat climate change and transform our energy system, move to energy efficiency and sustainable energy and impose a tax on carbon. It means that, in order to protect our water supply, we ban fracking. We must compete effectively in a global economy by making public colleges and universities tuition free and substantially reduce student debt.

Bernie Sanders Revolution

We must join the rest of the industrialized world and guarantee health care to all people as a right and not a privilege. We must end the disgrace of having more people in jail than any other country on earth and move toward real criminal justice reform at the federal, state and local levels. We must pass comprehensive immigration reform and provide a path toward citizenship for 11 million undocumented people. We must take a hard look at the waste, cost overruns and inefficiencies in every branch of government –including the Department of Defense. And we must make certain our brave young men and women in the military are not thrown into perpetual warfare in the Middle East or other wars we should not be fighting.
But the political revolution means much more than fighting for our ideals at the Democratic National Convention and defeating Donald Trump. It means that, at every level, we continue the fight to make our society a nation

Bernie Sanders Revolution

of economic, social, racial and environmental justice. It means that we can no longer ignore the fact that, sadly, the current Democratic Party leadership has turned its back on dozens of states in this country and has allowed right-wing politicians to win elections in some states with virtually no opposition including some of the poorest states in America. The Democratic Party needs a 50-state strategy. We may not win in every state tomorrow but we will never win unless we recruit good candidates and develop organizations that can compete effectively in the future. We must provide resources to those states which have so long been ignored. Most importantly, the Democratic Party needs leadership which is prepared to open its doors and welcome into its ranks working people and young people. That is the energy that we need to transform the Democratic Party, take on the special interests and transform our country. Here is a cold, hard

Bernie Sanders Revolution

fact that must be addressed. Since 2009, some 900 legislative seats have been lost to Republicans in state after state throughout this country. In fact, the Republican Party now controls 31 state legislatures and controls both the governors' mansions and statehouses in 23 states. That is unacceptable. We need to start engaging at the local and state level in an unprecedented way. Hundreds of thousands of volunteers helped us make political history during the last year. These are people deeply concerned about the future of our country and their own communities. Now we need many of them to start running for school boards, city councils, county commissions, state legislatures and governorships. State and local governments make enormously important decisions and we cannot allow right-wing Republicans to increasingly control them. I hope very much that many of you listening tonight are prepared to engage at that level. I have no doubt that with

Bernie Sanders Revolution

the energy and enthusiasm our campaign has shown that we can win significant numbers of local and state elections if people are prepared to become involved. I also hope people will give serious thought to running for statewide offices and the U.S. Congress. And when we talk about transforming America, it is not just about elections. Many of my Republican colleagues believe that government is the enemy, that we need to eviscerate and privatize virtually all aspects of government whether it is Social Security, Medicare, the VA, EPA, the Postal Service or public education. I strongly disagree. In a democratic civilized society, government must play an enormously important role in protecting all of us and our planet. But in order for government to work efficiently and effectively, we need to attract great and dedicated people from all walks of life. We need people who are dedicated to public service and can provide the services we need in a high

Bernie Sanders Revolution

quality and efficient way. When we talk about a Medicare-for-all health care program and the need to make sure all of our people have quality health care, it means that we need tens of thousands of new doctors, nurses, dentists, psychologists and other medical personnel who are prepared to practice in areas where people today lack access to that care. It means that we need hundreds of thousands of people to become childcare workers and teachers so that our young people will get the best education available in the world. It means that as we combat climate change and transform our energy system away from fossil fuels, we need scientists and engineers and entrepreneurs who will help us make energy efficiency, solar energy, wind energy, geothermal and other developing technologies as efficient and cost effective as possible. It means that as we rebuild our crumbling infrastructure, we need millions of skilled construction workers of all

Bernie Sanders Revolution

kinds. It means that when we talk about growing our economy and creating jobs, we need great business people who can produce and distribute the products and services we need in a way that respects their employees and the environment. In other words, we need a new generation of people actively involved in public service who are prepared to provide the quality of life the American people deserve. Let me conclude by once again thanking everyone who has helped in this campaign in one way or another. We have begun the long and arduous process of transforming America, a fight that will continue tomorrow, next week, next year and into the future. My hope is that when future historians look back and describe how our country moved forward into reversing the drift toward oligarchy, and created a government which represents all the people and not just the few, they will note that, to a significant degree, that effort began with the political revolution of 2016.

Bernie Sanders Revolution

July 12th 2016 Bernie Sanders Speech

Let me begin by thanking the 13 million
Americans who voted for me during the
Democratic primaries. Let me also thank the
people here in New Hampshire who gave us our
first big win and a special thanks to the people
of Vermont whose support for so many years
has sustained me. Let me also thank the
hundreds of thousands of volunteers in every
state in our country who worked so hard on our
campaign and the millions of our contributors
who showed the world that we could run a
successful national campaign based on small
individual contributions 2 1/2 million of them.
Together, we have begun a political revolution
to transform America and that revolution
continues. Together, we continue the fight to
create a government which represents all of us,
and not just the one percent a government
based on the principles of economic, social,
racial and environmental justice. I am proud of

Bernie Sanders Revolution

the campaign we ran here in New Hampshire and across the country. Our campaign won the primaries and caucuses in 22 states, and when the roll call at the Democratic National Convention in Philadelphia is announced it will show that we won almost 1,900 delegates. That is a lot of delegates, far more than almost anyone thought we could win. But it is not enough to win the nomination. Secretary Clinton goes into the convention with 389 more pledged delegates than we have and a lot more super delegates. Secretary Clinton has won the Democratic nominating process, and I congratulate her for that. She will be the Democratic nominee for president and I intend to do everything I can to make certain she will be the next president of the United States.

I have come here today not to talk about the past but to focus on the future. That future will be shaped more by what happens on November 8 in voting booths across our nation than by any

Bernie Sanders Revolution

other event in the world. I have come here to make it as clear as possible as to why I am endorsing Hillary Clinton and why she must become our next president. During the last year I had the extraordinary opportunity to speak to more than 1.4 million Americans at rallies in almost every state in this country. I was also able to meet with many thousands of other people at smaller gatherings. And the profound lesson that I have learned from all of that is that this campaign is not really about Hillary Clinton, or Donald Trump or Bernie Sanders, or any other candidate who sought the presidency. This campaign is about the needs of the American people and addressing the very serious crises that we face. And there is no doubt in my mind that, as we head into November, Hillary Clinton is far and away the best candidate to do that. It is easy to forget where we were seven and a half years ago when President Obama came into office. As a

Bernie Sanders Revolution

result of the greed, recklessness and illegal behavior on Wall Street, our economy was in the worst economic downturn since the Great Depression. Some 800,000 people a month were losing their jobs, we were running up a record-breaking deficit of $1.4 trillion dollars and the world's financial system was on the verge of collapse. We have come a long way in the last seven and a half years and I thank President Obama and Vice President Biden for their leadership in pulling us out of that terrible recession. But, I think we can all agree, much, much more needs to be done. Too many people in America are still being left out, left behind and ignored. In the richest country in the history of the world there is too much poverty, and too much despair. This election is about the single mom I saw in Nevada who, with tears in her eyes, told me that she was scared to death about the future because she and her young daughter were not making it on the $10.45 cents

Bernie Sanders Revolution

an hour she was earning. This election is about that woman, and the millions of other workers in this country who are falling further and further behind as they try to survive on totally inadequate wages. Hillary Clinton understands that we must fix an economy in America that is rigged and that sends almost all new wealth and income to the top one percent. Hillary Clinton understands that if someone in America works 40 hours a week, that person should not be living in poverty. She believes that we should raise the minimum wage to a living wage. And she wants to create millions of new jobs by rebuilding our crumbling infrastructure. – our roads, bridges, water systems and wastewater plants. But her opponent Donald Trump well, he has a very different view. He believes that states should have the right to lower the minimum wage or even abolish the concept of the minimum wage altogether. If Donald Trump is elected, we will see no increase in the federal

Bernie Sanders Revolution

minimum wage of $7.25 per hour a starvation wage. This election is about which candidate will nominate Supreme Court justices who are prepared to overturn the disastrous Citizens United decision which allows billionaires to buy elections and undermine our democracy; about who will appoint new justices on the Supreme Court who will defend a woman's right to choose, the rights of the LGBT community, workers' rights, the needs of minorities and immigrants, and the government's ability to protect the environment. If you don't believe this election is important, take a moment to think about the Supreme Court justices that Donald Trump will nominate, and what that means to civil liberties, equal rights and the future of our country. This campaign is about moving the United States toward universal health care and reducing the number of people who are uninsured or under-insured. Hillary Clinton wants to see that all Americans have the right to choose a public option in their health care exchange, which will lower the cost of health care. She also believes that anyone 55 years or older should be able to opt in to Medicare and she wants to see millions more Americans gain access to primary health care, dental care, mental health counseling and low-cost prescription drugs through a major expansion of community health centers throughout this country. Hillary is committed to seeing thousands of young doctors, nurses, psychologists, dentists and other medical professionals practice in underserved areas as we follow through on President Obama's idea of tripling funding for the National Health Service Corps. In New Hampshire, in Vermont and across the country we have a major epidemic of opiate and heroin addiction. People are dying every day from overdoses. Hillary Clinton understands that if we are serious about addressing this crisis we need major changes in

the way we deliver mental health treatment.
That's what expanding community health
centers will do and that is what getting medical
personnel into the areas we need them most will
do. And What is Donald Trump's position on
health care? No surprise there. Same old, same
old Republican contempt for working families.
He wants to abolish the Affordable Care Act,
throw 20 million people off of the health
insurance they currently have and cut Medicaid
for lower-income Americans. The last thing we
need today in America is a president who
doesn't care about whether millions will lose
access to the health care coverage that they
desperately need. We need more people with
access to quality health care, not fewer.
Hillary Clinton also understands that millions of
seniors, disabled vets and others are struggling
with the outrageously high cost of prescription
drugs. She and I are in agreement that
Medicare must negotiate drug prices with the

Bernie Sanders Revolution

pharmaceutical industry and that we must expand the use of generic medicine. Drug companies should not be making billions in profits while one in five Americans are unable to afford the medicine they need. The greed of the drug companies must end. This election is about the grotesque level of income and wealth inequality that currently exists, the worst it has been since 1928. Hillary Clinton knows that something is very wrong when the very rich become richer while many others are working longer hours for lower wages. She knows that it is absurd that middle-class Americans are paying an effective tax rate higher than hedge fund millionaires, and that there are corporations in this country making billions in profit while they pay no federal income taxes in a given year because of loopholes their lobbyists created. While Hillary Clinton supports making our tax code fairer, Donald Trump wants to give hundreds of billions of dollars in tax breaks to

Bernie Sanders Revolution

the very wealthiest people in this country. His reckless economic policies will not only exacerbate income and wealth inequality, they would increase our national debt by trillions of dollars. This election is about the thousands of young people I have met who have left college deeply in debt, the many others who cannot afford to go to college and the need for this country to have the best educated workforce in the world if we are to compete effectively in a highly competitive global economy. Hillary Clinton believes that we must substantially lower student debt, and that we must make public colleges and universities tuition free for the middle class and working families of this country. This is a major initiative that will revolutionize higher education in this country and improve the lives of millions. Think of what it will mean when every child in this country, regardless of the income of their family, knows that if they study hard and do well in school

Bernie Sanders Revolution

yes, they will be able to get a college education and leave school without debt. This election is about climate change, the greatest environmental crisis facing our planet, and the need to leave this world in a way that is healthy and habitable for our kids and future generations. Hillary Clinton is listening to the scientists who tell us that if we do not act boldly in the very near future there will be more drought, more floods, more acidification of the oceans, more rising sea levels. She understands that we must work with countries around the world in transforming our energy system away from fossil fuels and into energy efficiency and sustainable energy and that when we do that we can create a whole lot of good paying jobs. Donald Trump: Well, like most Republicans, he chooses to reject science something no presidential candidate should do. He believes that climate change is a hoax. In fact, he wants to expand the use of fossil fuel.

Bernie Sanders Revolution

That would be a disaster for our country and our planet. This election is about the leadership we need to pass comprehensive immigration reform and repair a broken criminal justice system. It's about making sure that young people in this country are in good schools or at good jobs, not in jail cells. Secretary Clinton understands that we don't need to have more people in jail than any other country on earth, at an expense of $80 billion a year. In these stressful times for our country, this election must be about bringing our people together, not dividing us up. While Donald Trump is busy insulting Mexicans, Muslims, women, African Americans and veterans, Hillary Clinton understands that our diversity is one of our greatest strengths. Yes. We become stronger when black and white, Latino, Asian American, Native American all of us stand together. Yes. We become stronger when men and women, young and old, gay and straight, native born and immigrant fight to rid this country of all forms of bigotry. It is no secret that Hillary Clinton and I disagree on a number of issues. That's what this campaign has been about. That's what democracy is about. But I am happy to tell you that at the Democratic Platform Committee which ended Sunday night in Orlando, there was a significant coming together between the two campaigns and we produced, by far, the most progressive platform in the history of the Democratic Party. Our job now is to see that platform implemented by a Democratic Senate, a Democratic House and a Hillary Clinton president and I am going to do everything I can to make that happen.

I have known Hillary Clinton for 25 years. I remember her as a great first lady who broke precedent in terms of the role that a first lady was supposed to play as she helped lead the fight for universal health care. I served with her in the United States Senate and know her as a fierce advocate for the rights of children.

Bernie Sanders Revolution

Hillary Clinton will make an outstanding president and I am proud to stand with her here today.

May 31, 2017 Bernie Sanders Speech

You know and I know that these are tough times for our country. But I do want to say that standing up here and looking out at the beautiful people in front of me, I have enormous confidence in the future of our country. Let me begin by congratulating the graduating class of 2017. Today is an important lives in your lives, something that I know you have worked very hard to achieve. And I want to wish all of you the very best of luck in your future endeavors. May I not be strangled. See, not only do I think you have a right to read on the grass, I think speakers have the right not to have that stuff around their throats. But I do want, on behalf of my wife Jan and myself, to see and pray that you all live happy and healthy lives, doing the

Bernie Sanders Revolution

work that you enjoy, surrounded in love by family and friends. And let me thank president Michelle Anderson, Nicole Haas, the Brooklyn College administration, faculty and staff, and all of you for inviting Jane and me back to Brooklyn, where we were both born and raised. And I am very honored by the honorary degree you have given me. I grew up in Flatbush, and like Senator Schumer, graduated from James Madison High School. My wife Jane was also raised in Flatbush and Bedford-Stuyvesant and graduated from Saint Xavier's high school, a few miles away from here. In 1959, as a first-generation college student, I attended Brooklyn College for a year, a year that had a major impact on my life. After that year I left for the University of Chicago, where I eventually graduated. My mom had died the previous year and I felt it was time to leave the neighborhood, and see what the rest of the world looked like.

Bernie Sanders Revolution

My childhood in Brooklyn was shaped by two profound realities. First, my mom, dad and older brother, who graduated from Brooklyn College, lived in a three-and-a-half-room rent-controlled apartment. As with many of your families who don't have a lot of money, financial pressure caused friction and tension within our household. From those experiences of growing up without a lot of money, I have never forgotten that there are millions of people throughout this country who struggle to put food on the table, pay the electric bill, try to save for their kids' education or for their retirement. People who against great odds are fighting today to live in dignity. The second reality that impacted my life was that my father left Poland at the age of 17, from a community that was not only very poor, but from a country where anti-Semitism, pogroms, and attacks on Jews were not uncommon. While my father immigrated to the United States and escaped Hitler and the

Bernie Sanders Revolution

Holocaust, many in his family did not. For them, racism, right-wing extremism and ultra-nationalism were not political issues. They were issues of life and death. And some of them died horrific deaths. From that experience, what was indelibly stamped on my mind was the understanding that we must never allow demagogues to divide us up by race, by religion, by national origin, by gender, or sexual orientation. Black and whites, Latino, Asian-American, Native American, Christian, Jew, Muslim and every religion. Straight or gay. Male or female. We must stand together. This country belongs to all of us. As the United States senator from Vermont, let me give you a very brief overview of the current crises we face. Crises which do not often get the attention they deserve. Just are not talked about. As a student at James Madison High School many years ago, I recall my social studies teacher talking about how there were small developing countries

around the world that were oligarchic societies.
Places where the economic and political life
nation were controlled by a handful of very
wealthy people. It never occurred to me as a kid
in Brooklyn that the United States of America,
our great nation, could move in that direction,
but that is precisely in my view what is
happening today. Today in America, the top
tenth of the 1 percent owns almost as wealth as
the bottom 90 percent. Twenty Americans now
own as much as the bottom half of America.
And one family now owns as much wealth as
the bottom 42 percent of our people. In the last
17 years, while the middle class continues to
decline, we have seen a tenfold increase in the
number of billionaires. Today in America are
earning almost 300 times what the average
worker makes. And in terms of income, while
you and your parents are working in some
cases two or three jobs, 52 percent of all new
income generated today goes to the top 1

percent. Meanwhile, at the same time as we have more income and wealth inequality than any other nation. Forty-three million Americans live in poverty. Half of older workers have nothing in the bank as they approach retirement. And in some inner cities and rural communities, youth unemployment is 20, 30, 40 percent. Unbelievably in our country today as a result of hopelessness and despair, we are seeing a decline in life expectancy. People are giving up and they're turning to drugs and alcohol. And even to suicide. And because of poverty and racism, today in a broken criminal justice system, we have more people in jail than any other country on earth. And those people are disproportionately black, Latino and Native American. Directly related to the oligarchic community we currently have is a corrupt political system which is undermining American democracy. And it's important we talk about and understand that. As a result of the disastrous

Bernie Sanders Revolution

Citizens United Supreme Court decision, corporations and billionaires are able to spend unlimited sums of money on elections and the result is today that a handful, a small number of billionaires are spending hundreds of millions of dollars every single year, often on ugly 30-second ads, helping to elect candidates who represent the wealthy and the powerful.
We are seeing how the results of how oligarchy functions right now, right now in Congress, where the Republican leadership wants to throw 23 million off of medical insurance, cut Medicaid by $800 billion, defund Planned Parenthood, cut food stamps and other nutrition programs by over $200 billion, cut Headstart and after-school programs. And by the way, make drastic in Pell grants and other programs that help working-class kids be able to go to college. And unbelievably, at exactly the same time as they are throwing people off of healthcare, making it harder for kids to go to college, they have the

Bernie Sanders Revolution

chutzpah to provide $300 billion in tax breaks to the top 1 percent. In other words, the very very rich are getting richer and they get tax breaks. The working class and middle class are struggling and they are seeing drastic cuts in life and death programs that could mean survival or not survival for those families. Now in response to these very serious crises it seems to me we have two choices. First, we can throw up our hands in despair. We can say the system is rigged, I am not going to get involved. That is understandable, but it is wrong. Because the issues that we deal with today the economic issues, the social issues, the racial issues, the environmental issues, not only impact your lives they impact the lives of future generations. And you do not have the moral right to turn your back on saving this planet and saving this future generations. The truth is that the only rational choice we have, the only real response we can make is to stand up and fight back, reclaim

Bernie Sanders Revolution

American democracy and create a government that works for all of us, not just the 1 percent. And for us to do that it is necessary that we fight for a vision of a new America. An America based on progressive, humane values, not the values of the oligarchy. And what does that mean? Briefly, in concrete terms: It means that no we aren't going to throw 23 million Americans off the healthcare they have. We are going to bring about healthcare for all as a right not a privilege. It means that no we are not, as the current administration does, the reality of climate change. No we are going to take on the fossil fuel industry, transform our energy system from fossil fuel to energy efficiency and sustainable energy. It means no we're not going to cut Pell grants and other student assistance. We are going to do what Germany, what Scandinavia, what countries all over the world do. And that is: to make certain that public colleges are tuition free. And we're going to

Bernie Sanders Revolution

significantly lower student debt because we believe that anyone in America who has the ability and the desire should be able to a get a higher education regardless of his or her income. And no we're not going to do what the attorney general of the United States now wants. We're not going to put more people in jail. We're going to fix a broken criminal justice system and invest in more jobs and education for our young people, not more jails and incarceration. No, we're not going to defund Planned Parenthood. We're going to vigorously defend a woman's right to choose.

My friends, let me conclude by saying this: We live in the wealthiest country in the history of the world. We are seeing an exploding technology which if used well has extraordinary potential to improve life. We are an intelligent and hardworking people. If we are prepared to stand together. If we take on greed and selfishness. If we refuse to allow demagogues to divide us up.

Bernie Sanders Revolution

There is no end to what the great people of our nation can accomplish. So today, as you graduate from Brooklyn College, my message to you is very simple: think big not small and help us create the nation we all know we can become.

October 9th, 2018 Bernie Sanders Speech

Thank you so much Dean Nasr for your introduction, to Johns Hopkins for inviting me here, and for all of you joining me here today, as well of those of you watching online. In the United States, we pay a whole lot of attention to issues impacting the economy, healthcare, education, environment, criminal justice, immigration and, as we have recently seen, Supreme Court nominees. These are all enormously important issues. With the exception of immediate and dramatic crises, however, foreign policy is not something that usually gets a whole lot of attention or debate. In

Bernie Sanders Revolution

fact, some political analysts have suggested that by and large we have a one-party foreign policy, where the basic elements of our approach are not often debated or challenged. We spend $700 billion a year on the military, more than the next 10 nations combined. We have been at war in Afghanistan for 17 years, war in Iraq for 15 years, and we are currently involved militarily in Yemen where a humanitarian crisis is taking place. Meanwhile, 30 million people have no health insurance, our infrastructure is collapsing, and hundreds of thousands of bright young people cannot afford to go to college every year.

The time is long overdue for a vigorous discussion about our foreign policy, and how it needs to change in this new era. Today, I want to say a few words about a troubling trend in global affairs that gets far too little attention. There is currently a struggle of enormous consequence taking place in the United States

Bernie Sanders Revolution

and throughout the world. In it we see two competing visions. On one hand, we see a growing worldwide movement toward authoritarianism, oligarchy, and kleptocracy. On the other side, we see a movement toward strengthening democracy, egalitarianism, and economic, social, racial, and environmental justice. This struggle has consequences for the entire future of the planet economically, socially, and environmentally. In terms of the global economy, we see today massive and growing wealth and income inequality, where the world's top one percent now owns more wealth than the bottom 99%, where a small number of huge financial institutions exert enormous impact over the lives of billions of people. Further, many people in industrialized countries are questioning whether democracy can actually deliver for them. They are working longer hours for lower wages than they used to. They see big money buying elections, and they see a political

Bernie Sanders Revolution

and economic elite growing wealthier, even as their own children's future grows dimmer.

In these countries, we often have political leaders who exploit these fears by amplifying resentments, stoking intolerance and fanning ethnic and racial hatreds among those who are struggling. We see this very clearly in our own country. It is coming from the highest level of our government. It should be clear by now that Donald Trump and the right-wing movement that supports him is not a phenomenon unique to the United States. All around the world, in Europe, in Russia, in the Middle East, in Asia, Latin America, and elsewhere we are seeing movements led by demagogues who exploit people's fears, prejudices and grievances to gain and hold on to power. Just this past weekend, in Brazil's presidential election, right-wing leader Jair Bolsonaro, who has been called "The Donald Trump of Brazil," made a very strong showing in the first round of voting, coming up just short of an outright victory. Bolsonaro has a long record of attacks against immigrants, against minorities, against women, against LGBT people. Bolsonaro, who has said he loves Donald Trump, has praised Brazil's former military dictatorship, and has said, among other things, that in order to deal with crime, police should simply be allowed to shoot more criminals. This is the person who may soon lead the world's fifth most populous country, and its ninth largest economy. Meanwhile, Brazil's most popular politician, the former president Lula da Silva, is imprisoned on highly questionable charges, and prevented from running again. Bolsonaro in Brazil is one example, there are others which I will discuss. But I think it is important that we understand that what we are seeing now in the world is the rise of a new authoritarian axis. While the leaders who make up this axis may differ in some respects, they share key attributes: intolerance

Bernie Sanders Revolution

toward ethnic and religious minorities, hostility toward democratic norms, antagonism toward a free press, constant paranoia about foreign plots, and a belief that the leaders of government should be able use their positions of power to serve their own selfish financial interests. Interestingly, many of these leaders are also deeply connected to a network of multi-billionaire oligarchs who see the world as their economic plaything. Those of us who believe in democracy, who believe that a government must be accountable to its people and not the other way around, must understand the scope of this challenge if we are to confront it effectively. We need to counter oligarchic authoritarianism with a strong global progressive movement that speaks to the needs of working people, that recognizes that many of the problems we are faced with are the product of a failed status quo. We need a movement that unites people all over the world who don't just seek to return to a

Bernie Sanders Revolution

romanticized past, a past that did not work for so many, but who strive for something better. While this authoritarian trend certainly did not begin with Donald Trump, there's no question that other authoritarian leaders around the world have drawn inspiration from the fact that the president of the world's oldest and most powerful democracy is shattering democratic norms, is viciously attack an independent media and an independent judiciary, and is scapegoating the weakest and most vulnerable members of our society. For example, Saudi Arabia is a country clearly inspired by Trump. This is a despotic dictatorship that does not tolerate dissent, that treats women as third-class citizens, and has spent the last several decades exporting a very extreme form of Islam around the world. Saudi Arabia is currently devastating the country of Yemen in a catastrophic war in alliance with the United States. I would like to take a moment to note the disappearance of

Bernie Sanders Revolution

Saudi journalist Jamal Khashoggi, a critic of the Saudi government who was last seen entering the Saudi consulate in Istanbul, Turkey, last Tuesday. Over the weekend, Turkish authorities told reporters that they now believe Khashoggi was murdered in the Saudi consulate, and his body disposed of elsewhere. We need to know what happened here. If this is true, if the Saudi regime murdered a journalist critic in their own consulate, there must be accountability, and there must be an unequivocal condemnation by the United States. But it seems clear that Saudi Crown Prince Mohammad bin Salman feels emboldened by the Trump administration's unquestioning support. Further, it is hard to imagine that a country like Saudi Arabia would have chosen to start a fight this past summer with Canada over a relatively mild human rights criticism if Muhammad bin Salman who is very close with Presidential son-in-law Jared Kushner did not believe that the United States

Bernie Sanders Revolution

would stay silent. Three years ago, who would have imagined that the United States would refuse to take sides between Canada, our democratic neighbor and second largest trading partner, and Saudi Arabia on an issue of human rights but that is exactly what happened.

It's also hard to imagine that Israel's Netanyahu government would have taken a number of steps including passing the recent "Nation State law," which essentially codifies the second-class status of Israel's non-Jewish citizens, aggressively undermining the longstanding goal of a two-state solution, and ignoring the economic catastrophe in Gaza if Netanyahu wasn't confident that Trump would support him. And then there is Trump's cozy relationship with Russian President Vladimir Putin, whose intervention in our 2016 presidential election Trump still fails to fully admit. We face an unprecedented situation of an American president who for whatever reason refuses to acknowledge this attack on American democracy. Why is that? I am not sure what the answer is. Either he really doesn't understand what has happened, or he is under Russian influence because of compromising information they may have on him, or because he is ultimately more sympathetic to Russia's strongman form of government than he is to American democracy. Even as he draws closer to authoritarian leaders like Putin, like Orban in Hungary, Erdogan in Turkey, Duterte in the Philippines, and North Korea's Kim Jong Un, Trump is needlessly increasing tensions with our democratic European allies over issues like trade, like NATO, like the Iran nuclear agreement. Let me be clear, these are important issues. But the way Trump has gratuitously disrespected these allies is not only ineffective deal-making, it will have enormous negative long-term consequences for the trans-Atlantic alliance. Further, Trump's ambassador to

Bernie Sanders Revolution

Germany, Richard Grenell, several months ago made clear the administration's support for right-wing extremist parties across Europe. In other words, the U.S. administration is openly siding with the very forces challenging the democratic foundations of our longtime allies. We need to understand that the struggle for democracy is bound up with the struggle against kleptocracy and corruption. That is true here in the United States as well as abroad. In addition to Trump's hostility toward democratic institutions here in the United States, we have a billionaire president who, according to a recent report in the New York Times, acquired his wealth through illegal means, and now, as president, in an unprecedented way, has blatantly embedded his own economic interests and those of his cronies into the policies of government. One of the consistent themes of reports coming out of the investigation into the Trump campaign is the effort of wealthy foreign interests seeking

Bernie Sanders Revolution

influence and access with Trump and his organization, and with close Trump associates seeking to trade that access for the promise of even more wealth. While the characters involved in these reports are particularly blatant and clumsy in their efforts, the details of these stories are not unique. Never before have we seen the power of big money over governmental policy so clearly. Whether we're talking about the Koch brothers spending hundreds of millions of dollars to dismantle environmental regulations that protect Americans' health, or authoritarian monarchies like Saudi Arabia, the United Arab Emirates, and Qatar spending millions in fossil fuel wealth in Washington to advance the interests of their undemocratic regimes, or giant corporations supporting think tanks in order to produce policy recommendations that serve their own financial interests, the theme is the same. Powerful special interests use their wealth to influence government for their own

Bernie Sanders Revolution

selfish interests. During the Congressional fight over the Republicans' massive tax giveaway to the wealthy, some of my colleagues were very open this. Senator Lindsey Graham of South Carolina was very frank: If Republicans failed to pass the bill, he said "the financial contributions will stop." This, he went on, "will be the end of us as a party." I applaud Senator Graham for his honesty. This corruption is so blatant, it's no longer seen as remarkable. Just the other day, the lead sentence in a New York Times story about Republican mega-donor Sheldon Adelson was this: "The return on investment for many of the Republican Party's biggest political patrons has been less than impressive this year."

Let me repeat that: "The return on investment was less than impressive." The idea that political donors expect a specific policy result in exchange for their contributions a quid pro quo, the definition of corruption is right out there in the open. It is no longer even seen as

Bernie Sanders Revolution

scandalous. This sort of corruption is common among authoritarian regimes. In Russia, it is impossible to tell where the decisions of government end and the interests of Putin and his circle of multi-billionaire oligarchs begin. They operate as one unit. Similarly, in Saudi Arabia, there is no debate about separation because the natural resources of the state, valued at trillions of dollars, belong to the Saudi royal family. In Hungary, far-right authoritarian-nationalist leader Victor Orban models himself after Putin in Russia, saying in a January interview that, "Putin has made his country great again." Like Putin, Orban has risen to power by exploiting paranoia and intolerance of minorities, including outrageous anti-Semitic attacks on George Soros, but at the same time has managed to enrich his political allies and himself. In February, the Corruption Perception Index compiled by Transparency International ranked Hungary as the second most corrupt EU country. We must understand that these authoritarians are part of a common front. They are in close contact with each other, share tactics and, as in the case of European and American right-wing movements, even share some of the same funders. For example, the Mercer family, supporters of the infamous Cambridge Analytica, have also been key backers of Donald Trump and of Breitbart news, which operates in Europe, the United States and Israel to advance the same anti-immigrant, anti-Muslim agenda. Sheldon Adelson gives generously to the Republican Party and right-wing causes in both the United States and Israel, promoting a shared agenda of intolerance and bigotry in both countries.

The truth is, however, that to effectively oppose right-wing authoritarianism, we cannot simply be on the defensive. We need to be proactive and understand that just defending the failed status quo of the last several decades is not good enough. In fact, we need to recognize that the challenges we face today are a product of that status quo. What do I mean by that? Here in the United States, in the UK, in France, and in many other countries around the world, people are working longer hours for stagnating wages, and worry that their children will have a lower standard of living than they do. So our job is not to accept the status quo, not to accept massive levels of wealth and income inequality where the top 1% of the world's population own half the planet's wealth, while the bottom 70% of the working age population account for just 2.7% of global wealth. It is not to accept a declining standard of living for many workers around the world, not to accept a reality of 1.4 billion people living in extreme poverty where millions of children die of easily preventable illnesses. Our job is to fight for a future in which public policy and new technology and innovation work to benefit all of the people, not just the few.

Bernie Sanders Revolution

Our job is to support governments around the world that will end the absurdity of the rich and multinational corporations stashing over $21 trillion dollars in offshore bank accounts to avoid paying their fair share of taxes, and then demanding that their respective governments impose an austerity agenda on their working families. Our job is to rally the entire planet to stand up to the fossil fuel industry which continues to make huge profits while their carbon emissions destroy the planet for our children and grandchildren. The scientific community is virtually unanimous in telling us that climate change is real, climate change is caused by human activity, and climate change is already causing devastating harm throughout the world. Further, what the scientists tell us is that if we do not act boldly to address the climate crisis, this planet will see more drought, more floods, more extreme weather disturbances, more acidification of the ocean,

Bernie Sanders Revolution

more rising sea levels, and, as a result of mass migrations, there will be more threats to global stability and security. A new report from the United Nations Intergovernmental Panel on Climate Change released just yesterday warns that we only have about twelve years to take urgent and unprecedented action to prevent a rise in the planet's temperature that would cause irreversible damage. The threat of climate change is a very clear example of where American leadership can make a difference. Europe can't do it alone, China can't do it alone, and the United States can't do it alone. This is a crisis that calls out for strong international cooperation if we are to leave our children and grandchildren a planet that is healthy and habitable. American leadership the economic and scientific advantages and incentives that only America can offer is hugely important for facilitating this effort. In the struggle to preserve and expand democracy, our job is to fight back

Bernie Sanders Revolution

against the coordinated effort, strongly supported by the president and funded by oligarchs like the Koch brothers, to make it harder to for American citizens – often people of color, poor people, and young people – to vote. Not only do oligarchs want to buy elections, but voter suppression is a key element of their plan to maintain power. Our job is to push for trade policies that don't just benefit large multinational corporations and hurt working people throughout the world as they are written out of public view. Our job is to fight back against brutal immigration policies that require separating migrant families when they are detained at the border, and require children to be put in cages. Migrants and refugees should be treated with compassion and respect when they reach Europe or the United States. Yes, we need better international cooperation to address the flow of migrants across borders, but the solution is not to build walls and amplify the

Bernie Sanders Revolution

cruelty toward those fleeing impossible conditions as a deterrence strategy.

Our job is to make sure that we commit more resources to taking care of people than we do on weapons designed to kill them. It is not acceptable that, with the Cold War long behind us, countries around the world spend over a trillion dollars a year on weapons of destruction, while millions of children die of easily treatable diseases. According to the Stockholm International Peace Research Institute, countries around the world spend a total of $1.7 trillion a year on the military. $1.7 trillion. Think of what we could accomplish if even a fraction of this amount were redirected to more peaceful ends? The head of the United Nations Food and Agriculture Organization has said we could end the global food crisis for $30 billion a year. That's less than two percent of what we spend on weapons. Columbia University's Jeffrey Sachs, one of the world's leading experts on

Bernie Sanders Revolution

economic development and the fight against poverty, has estimated that the cost to end world poverty is $175 billion per year for 20 years, about ten percent of what the world spends on weapons. Donald Trump thinks we should spend more on these weapons. I think we should spend less. Let us remember what President Dwight D. Eisenhower said in 1953, just a few months after taking office. "Every gun that is made, every warship launched, every rocket fired signifies, in the final sense, a theft from those who hunger and are not fed, those who are cold and are not clothed. This world in arms is not spending money alone. It is spending the sweat of its laborers, the genius of its scientists, the hopes of its children." And just as he was about to leave office in 1961, Eisenhower was so concerned the growing power of the weapons industry that he issued this warning: "In the councils of government, we must guard against the acquisition of

Bernie Sanders Revolution

unwarranted influence, whether sought or unsought, by the military industrial complex. The potential for the disastrous rise of misplaced power exists and will persist." We have seen that potential more than fulfilled over the past decades. It is time for us to stand up and say: There is a better way to use our wealth.

In closing, let me simply that in order to effectively combat the forces of global oligarchy and authoritarianism, we need an international movement that mobilizes behind a vision of shared prosperity, security and dignity for all people, and that addresses the massive global inequality that exists, not only in wealth but in political power. Such a movement must be willing to think creatively and boldly about the world that we would like to see. While the authoritarian axis is committed to tearing down a post-World War II global order that they see as limiting their access to power and wealth, it is not enough for us to simply defend that order as it exists. We must look honestly at how that order has failed to deliver on many of its promises, and how authoritarians have adeptly exploited those failures in order to build support for their agenda. We must take the opportunity to re-conceptualize a global order based on human solidarity, an order that recognizes that every person on this planet shares a common humanity, that we all want our children to grow up healthy, to have a good education, have decent jobs, drink clean water, breathe clean air and to live in peace. Our job is to reach out to those in every corner of the world who shares these values, and who are fighting for a better world. Authoritarians seek power by promoting division and hatred. We will promote unity and inclusion. In a time of exploding wealth and technology, we have the potential to create a decent life for all people. Our job is to build on our common humanity and do everything that we can to oppose all of the forces, whether unaccountable government power or unaccountable corporate power, who try to divide us up and set us against each other. We know that those forces work together across borders. We must do the same.

March 2nd, 2019 Bernie Sanders Speech

Thank you all very much for being here today and thank you for being part of a political revolution which will transform America. Thank you for being part of a campaign which is not only going to win the Democratic nomination, which is not only going to defeat Donald Trump, the most dangerous president in modern American history, but with your help is going to transform this country and, finally, create an economy and government which works for all Americans, and not just the one percent. Today, I want to welcome you to a campaign which says, loudly and clearly, that the underlying principles of our government will

Bernie Sanders Revolution

not be greed, hatred and lies. It will not be racism, sexism, xenophobia, homophobia and religious bigotry. That is going to end. The principles of our government will be based on justice: economic justice, social justice, racial justice and environmental justice. Today, I want to welcome you to a campaign which tells the powerful special interests who control so much of our economic and political life that we will no longer tolerate the greed of corporate America and the billionaire class greed which has resulted in this country having more income and wealth inequality than any other major country on earth. No. We will no longer stand idly by and allow 3 people in this country to own more wealth than the bottom half of America while, at the same time, over 20 percent of our children live in poverty, veterans sleep out on the streets and seniors cannot afford their prescription drugs. We will no longer accept 46 percent of all new income going to the top 1 percent, while

Bernie Sanders Revolution

millions of Americans are forced to work 2 or 3
jobs just to survive and over half of our people
live paycheck to paycheck, frightened to death
about what happens to them financially if their
car breaks down or their child becomes sick.
Today, we fight for a political revolution.
We say to the private health insurance
companies, whether you like it or not, the United
States will join every other major country on
earth and guarantee healthcare to all people as
a right. All Americans are entitled to go to the
doctor when they're sick and not go bankrupt
after staying in the hospital. Yes. We will pass a
Medicare for all single-payer program.
Today, we say to the pharmaceutical industry,
that you will no longer charge the American
people the highest prices in the world for
prescription drugs, the result being that one out
of five Americans cannot afford the prescriptions
their doctors prescribe. The outrageous greed of
the pharmaceutical industry is going to end. We

Bernie Sanders Revolution

are going to lower prescription drug prices in this country. Today, we say to WalMart, the fast food industry and other low wage employers: Stop paying your employees starvation wages.. Yes. We are going to raise the federal minimum wage to a living wage $15 an hour. Nobody who works 40 hours a week in this country should live in poverty. And yes. We're going to make it easier for people to join unions, not harder. And by the way. Today we say to corporate America that artificial intelligence and robotics are not going to be used just to throw workers out on the street. This exploding technology must serve human needs, not just corporate profits. Today we say to the American people that we will rebuild our crumbling infrastructure: our roads, our bridges, our rail system and subways, our water systems and wastewater plants and our airports – and when we do that we create up to 13 million good paying jobs. Today we say to the parents in this country that you and your

Bernie Sanders Revolution

kids deserve quality, affordable childcare. The children are our future, and they deserve the best possible head start in life with a high quality, universal pre-K program.

Today, we say to our young people that we want you to get the best education that you can, regardless of the income of your family. Good jobs require a good education. That is why we are going to make public colleges and universities tuition free, and substantially lower the outrageous level of student debt that currently exists. America once had the best educated workforce in the world, and we are going to make that happen again. Today, we say to our senior citizens, that we understand that you cannot live in dignity when you are trying to survive on $13,000 or $14,000 a year in Social Security benefits. My Republican colleagues want to cut Social Security but we have some bad news for them. We're not going to cut Social Security benefits. We're going to

Bernie Sanders Revolution

expand them. Today, we say to Donald Trump and the fossil fuel industry that climate change is not a hoax but is an existential threat to our country and the entire planet – and we intend to transform our energy system away from fossil fuel and into energy efficiency and sustainable energy and, in the process, create millions of good paying jobs. All of us have a moral responsibility to make certain that the planet we leave to our children and grandchildren is healthy and habitable.

Today, we say to the prison-industrial-complex that we are going to bring about real criminal justice reform. We are going to end the international embarrassment of having more people in jail than any other country on earth. Instead of spending $80 billion a year on jails and incarceration, we are going to invest in jobs and education for our young people. No more private prisons and detention centers. No more profiteering from locking people up. No more

Bernie Sanders Revolution

"war on drugs." No more keeping people in jail because they're too poor to afford cash bail. And by the way, when we talk about criminal justice reform, we're going to change a system in which tens of thousands of Americans every year get criminal records for possessing marijuana, but not one major Wall Street executive went to jail for destroying our economy in 2008 as a result of their greed, recklessness and illegal behavior. No. They didn't go to jail. They got a trillion-dollar bailout. Today, we say to the American people that instead of demonizing the undocumented immigrants in this country, we're going to pass comprehensive immigration reform and provide a path toward citizenship. We're going to provide legal status to the 1.8 million young people eligible for the DACA program, and develop a humane border policy for those who seek asylum. No more snatching babies from the arms of their mothers. Today, we say to the

Bernie Sanders Revolution

top 1 percent and the large profitable corporations in this country people who have never had it so good that under a Bernie Sanders administration we're going to end the massive tax breaks and loopholes that you currently enjoy. We will no longer accept the absurd situation where large corporations like Amazon, Netflix and General Motors pay nothing in federal income taxes after raking in billions in profits. We will no longer tolerate the situation in which the wealthy and large corporations stash billions in tax havens throughout the world. Yes, the wealthy and multi-national corporations in this country will start paying their fair share of taxes. We are going to end austerity for working families, and provide some austerity for large, multi-national corporations. Today, we say to the military-industrial-complex that we will not continue to spend $700 billion a year on the military more than the next ten nations combined. We're going

Bernie Sanders Revolution

to invest in affordable housing, we're going to invest in public education, we're going to invest in rebuilding our crumbling infrastructure – not more nuclear weapons and never-ending wars. Brothers and sisters: We're going to win this election not because we have a super PAC funded by billionaires. We're going to win this election because we will put together the strongest grassroots coalition in the history of American politics. Donald Trump wants to divide us up by the color of our skin, our country of origin, our gender, our religion and our sexual orientation. We are going to do exactly the opposite. We are going to bring our people together black, white, Latino, Native American, Asian American, gay and straight, young and old, men and women, native born and immigrant. We are going to bring our people together for an unprecedented grassroots effort, which, I am happy to tell you, already has over one million people signed up as volunteers.

Bernie Sanders Revolution

If I might, as I return here to Brooklyn, let me take a moment to become personal. As we launch this campaign for president, you deserve to know where I come from because family history heavily influences the values that we adopt as adults. I was born and raised a few miles away from here, in a three-and-a-half room rent-controlled apartment. My father was a paint salesman who worked hard his entire life, but never made much money. My mother raised my brother and me. I learned a great deal about immigration as a child because my father came to this country from Poland at the age of 17, without a nickel in his pocket. He came to escape the crushing poverty that existed in his community, and to escape widespread anti-Semitism. And, it was a good thing that he left Poland when he did because virtually his entire family there was wiped out by Nazi barbarism. I am not going to tell you that I grew up in a home of desperate poverty. That would not be

Bernie Sanders Revolution

true. But what I will tell you is that coming from a lower middle class family I will never forget how money or really lack of money was always a point of stress in our home. My mother's dream was that someday our family would move out of that rent-controlled apartment to a home of our own. That dream was never fulfilled. She died young while we were still living in that rent-controlled apartment. My experience as a kid, living in a family that struggled economically, powerfully influenced my life and my values. Unlike Donald Trump, who shut down the government and left 800,000 federal employees without income to pay the bills, I know what it's like to be in a family that lives paycheck to paycheck. Now it's true: I did not have a father who gave me millions of dollars to build luxury skyscrapers, casinos and country clubs. I did not come from a family that gave me a $200,000 allowance every year beginning at the age of 3. As I recall, my allowance was 25 cents a week.

Bernie Sanders Revolution

But I had something more valuable: I had the role model of a father who had unbelievable courage in journeying across an ocean, with no money in his pocket, to start a new and better life. I did not come from a family of privilege that prepared me to entertain people on television by telling workers: "You're fired." I came from a family who knew all too well the frightening power employers can have over everyday workers. I did not come from a politically connected family whose multinational corporation got special tax breaks and subsidies. I came from a family where my parents paid their taxes and understood the important role that government plays in a democracy. I did not come from a family that could afford to send my brother and me to an elite boarding school. In fact, I was educated in high quality public schools here in Brooklyn and began the first year of my college life on this

Bernie Sanders Revolution

very campus. I should also mention that my brother graduated from Brooklyn College. Having attended an excellent public college that was then virtually tuition free and living in a rent-controlled apartment, I can assure you that my family believed that government in a democratic society had a very important role to play in protecting working families. I did not come from a family that taught me to build a corporate empire through housing discrimination. I protested housing discrimination, was arrested for protesting school segregation, and attended Reverend Dr. Martin Luther King's March on Washington for jobs and freedom.

Brothers and sisters. Over the last two years, and before, you and I and millions of Americans have stood up and fought for justice in every part of our society. And we've had some successes. Together, as billionaires and large corporations have attacked unions, destroyed

Bernie Sanders Revolution

pensions, deregulated the banks, and slashed wages, we have succeeded in raising the minimum wage to $15 in states and cities across the country. And forced large corporations like Amazon and Disney to do the same. And we have supported teachers who successfully stood up for their kids in strike after strike after strike. Together, as the forces of militarism have kept us engaged in unending wars, we have stood arm-in-arm to fight back. For the first time in 45 years, we have utilized the War Powers Act to move us forward in ending the horrific Saudi-led war in Yemen.

Together, as so many of our young people have received criminal records for nonviolent offenses, we have fought to end the war on drugs, and have seen state after state decriminalize marijuana, and have seen communities expunge the criminal records of those arrested on these charges. Let's be

Bernie Sanders Revolution

honest: while we have won some victories, our struggles have not always been successful. But I am here to tell you, that because of all the work we have done, we are now on the brink of winning not just an election, but transforming our country. And let me tell you what that means. When We are in the White House, we will enact a federal jobs guarantee, to ensure that everyone is guaranteed a stable job. There is more than enough work to be done in this country. Let's do it. When We are in the White House we will attack the problem of urban gentrification and build the affordable housing our nation desperately needs.

When We are in he White House we will end the decline of rural America, reopen those rural hospitals that have been closed, and make sure that our young people have decent jobs so they do not have to leave the towns they grew up in and love. When We are in he White House, we will move aggressively to end the epidemic of

Bernie Sanders Revolution

gun violence in this country and pass the common sense gun safety legislation that the overwhelming majority of Americans want. People who should not have guns, will not have guns. When We are in the White House, we are going to address not only the disparities of wealth and income that exist overall in our nation, but we will address the racial disparities of wealth and income. We are going to root out institutional racism wherever it exists. Not only will we end voter suppression, we are going to make it easier for people to vote – not harder.

When We are in the White House, we are going to protect a woman's right to control her own body. That is her decision, not the government's. Make no mistake about it, this struggle is not just about defeating Donald Trump. This struggle is about taking on the incredibly powerful institutions that control the economic and political life of this country. And

Bernie Sanders Revolution

I'm talking about Wall Street, the insurance companies, the drug companies, the military-industrial complex, the prison-industrial complex, the fossil fuel industry and a corrupt campaign finance system that enables billionaires to buy elections. Brothers and sisters: We have an enormous amount of work in front of us. And this what I believe. If we stand together, if we don't allow Trump and his friends to divide us up, there is nothing we cannot accomplish.

This country has an extraordinary future. Let's make it happen.

July 11th, 2019 Bernie Sanders Speech
My friends, we are in the midst of a defining and pivotal moment for our country and our planet. And, with so many crises converging upon us simultaneously, it is easy for us to become overwhelmed or depressed or to even throw up our hands in resignation. But my message to

Bernie Sanders Revolution

you today is that if there was ever a moment in the history of our country where despair was not an option, this is that time. If there was ever a moment where we had to effectively analyze the competing political and social forces which define this historical period, this is that time. If there was ever a moment when we needed to stand up and fight against the forces of oligarchy and authoritarianism, this is that time. And, if there was ever a moment when we needed a new vision to bring our people together in the fight for justice, decency and human dignity, this is that time. In the year 2019 the United States and the rest of the world face two very different political paths. On one hand, there is a growing movement towards oligarchy and authoritarianism in which a small number of incredibly wealthy and powerful billionaires own and control a significant part of the economy and exert enormous influence over the political life of our country. On the other hand, in

Bernie Sanders Revolution

opposition to oligarchy, there is a movement of working people and young people who, in ever increasing numbers, are fighting for justice. They are the teachers taking to the streets to make certain that schools are adequately funded and that their students get a quality education. They are workers at Disney, Amazon, Walmart and the fast food industry standing up and fighting for a living wage of at least $15 an hour and the right to have a union.

They are young people taking on the fossil fuel industry and demanding policies that transform our energy system and protect our planet from the ravages of climate change. They are women who refuse to give control of their bodies to local, state and federal politicians.
They are people of color and their allies demanding an end to systemic racism and massive racial inequities that exist throughout our society. They are immigrants and their allies

Bernie Sanders Revolution

fighting to end the demonization of undocumented people and for comprehensive immigration reform. When we talk about oligarchy, let us be clear about what we mean. Right now, in the United States of America, three families control more wealth than the bottom half of our country, some 160 million Americans. The top 1% own more wealth than the bottom 92% and 49% of all new income generated today goes to the top 1%. In fact, income and wealth inequality today in the United States is greater than at any time since the 1920s. And when we talk about oligarchy, it is not just that the very rich are getting much richer. It is that tens of millions of working-class people, in the wealthiest country on earth, are suffering under incredible economic hardship, desperately trying to survive. Today, nearly 40 million Americans live in poverty and tonight, 500,000 people will be sleeping out on the streets. About half of the country lives paycheck

Bernie Sanders Revolution

to paycheck as tens of millions of our people are an accident, a divorce, a sickness or a layoff away from economic devastation. While many public schools throughout the country lack the resources to adequately educate our young people, we are the most heavily incarcerated nation on earth. After decades of policies that have encouraged and subsidized unbridled corporate greed, we now have an economy that is fundamentally broken and grotesquely unfair. Even while macroeconomic numbers like GDP, the stock market and the unemployment rate are strong, millions of middle class and working people struggle to keep their heads above water, while the billionaire class consumes the lion's share of the wealth that we are collectively creating as a nation. In the midst of a so-called booming economy real wages for the average worker have barely risen at all. And despite an explosion in technology and worker productivity, the average wage of the American worker in

Bernie Sanders Revolution

real dollars is no higher than it was 46 years ago and millions of people are forced to work two or three jobs just to survive. And here is something quite incredible that tells you all you need to know about the results of unfettered capitalism. All of us want to live long, happy, and productive lives but. in America today the very rich live on average 15 years longer than the poorest Americans.

In 2014, in McDowell County, West Virginia, one of the poorest counties in the nation, life expectancy for men was 64 years. In Fairfax County, Virginia, a wealthy county, just 350 miles away, life expectancy for men was nearly 82 years, an 18-year differential. The life expectancy gap for women in the two counties was 12 years. In other words, the issue of unfettered capitalism is not just an academic debate, poverty, economic distress and despair are life-threatening issues for millions of working

Bernie Sanders Revolution

people in the country. While the rich get richer they live longer lives. While poor and working families struggle economically and often lack adequate health care, their life expectancy is declining for the first time in modern American history. Taken together, the American Dream of upward mobility is in peril. In fact, if we don't turn things around, our younger generation will, for the first time in living memory, have a lower standard of living than their parents. This is not acceptable. Globally, the situation is even more shocking with most of the world's wealth concentrated among a very few, while billions of people have almost nothing. Today, the world's richest 26 billionaires now own as much wealth as the poorest 3.8 billion people on the planet – half of the world's population. But the struggle we are facing today is not just economic. Across the globe, the movement toward oligarchy runs parallel to the growth of authoritarian regimes – like Putin in Russia, Xi in

Bernie Sanders Revolution

China, Mohamed Bin Salman in Saudi Arabia, Rodrigo Duterte in the Philippines, Jair Bolsonaro in Brazil, and Viktor Orbán in Hungary among others. These leaders meld corporatist economics with xenophobia and authoritarianism. They redirect popular anger about inequality and declining economic conditions into violent rage against minorities whether they are immigrants, racial minorities, religious minorities or the LGBT community. And to suppress dissent, they are cracking down on democracy and human rights. In the United States, of course, we have our own version of this movement – which is being led by President Trump and many of his Republican allies who are attempting to divide our country up and attack these same communities. How sad it is that President Trump sees these authoritarian leaders as friends and allies. This authoritarian playbook is not new. The challenge we confront today as a nation, and as a world, is in many

Bernie Sanders Revolution

ways not different from the one we faced a little less than a century ago, during and after the Great Depression in the 1930s. Then, as now, deeply-rooted and seemingly intractable economic and social disparities led to the rise of right-wing nationalist forces all over the world. In Europe, the anger and despair was ultimately harnessed by authoritarian demagogues who fused corporatism, nationalism, racism and xenophobia into a political movement that amassed totalitarian power, destroyed democracy, and ultimately murdering millions of people including members of my own family. But we must remember that those were not the only places where dark forces tried to rise up. Today, we are all rightly repulsed by the sight of neo-Nazis and Klansmen openly marching in Charlottesville, VA, and we are horrified by houses of worship being shot up by right-wing terrorists. But on February 20, 1939, over 20,000 Nazis held a mass rally not in Berlin, not

Bernie Sanders Revolution

in Rome, but in Madison Square Garden, in front of a 30-foot-tall banner of George Washington bordered with swastikas in New York City. But back then, those American extremists could not replicate the success of their authoritarian brethren across the ocean because we in the United States, thankfully, made a different choice than Europe did in responding to the era's social and economic crises. We rejected the ideology of Mussolini and Hitler we instead embraced the bold and visionary leadership of President Franklin Delano Roosevelt, then the leader of the progressive wing of the Democratic Party. Together with organized labor, leaders in the African American community and progressives inside and outside the Party, Roosevelt led a transformation of the American government and the American economy. Like today, the quest for transformative change was opposed by big business, Wall Street, the political

Bernie Sanders Revolution

establishment, by the Republican Party and by the conservative wing of FDR's own Democratic Party. And he faced the same scare tactics then that we experience today red baiting, xenophobia, racism and anti-Semitism. In a famous 1936 campaign speech Roosevelt stated, "We had to struggle with the old enemies of peace–business and financial monopoly, speculation, reckless banking, class antagonism, sectionalism, war profiteering. They had begun to consider the government of the United States as a mere appendage to their own affairs. We know now that government by organized money is just as dangerous as government by organized mob". Never before in all our history have these forces been so united against one candidate as they stand today. They are unanimous in their hate for me and I welcome their hatred. Despite that opposition, by rallying the American people, FDR and his progressive coalition created the New Deal, won four terms, and created an economy that worked for all and not just the few. Today, New Deal initiatives like Social Security, unemployment compensation, the right to form a union, the minimum wage, protection for farmers, regulation of Wall Street and massive infrastructure improvements are considered pillars of American society. But, while he stood up for the working families of our country, we can never forget that President Roosevelt was reviled by the oligarchs of his time, who berated these extremely popular programs as "socialism." Similarly, in the 1960s, when Lyndon Johnson brought about Medicare, Medicaid and other extremely popular programs, he was also viciously attacked by the ruling class of this country. And here is the point. It is no exaggeration to state, that not only did FDR's agenda improve the lives of millions of Americans, but the New Deal was enormously popular politically and helped defeat

Bernie Sanders Revolution

far-right extremism. For a time. Today, America and the world are once again moving towards authoritarianism and the same right-wing forces of oligarchy, corporatism, nationalism, racism and xenophobia are on the march, pushing us to make the apocalyptically wrong choice that Europe made in the last century. Today, we now see a handful of billionaires with unprecedented wealth and power. We see huge private monopolies operating outside of any real democratic oversight and often subsidized by taxpayers with the power to control almost every aspect of our lives. They are the profit-taking gatekeepers of our health care, our technology, our finance system, our food supply and almost all of the other basic necessities of life. They are Wall Street, the insurance companies, the drug companies, the fossil fuel industry, the military industrial complex, the prison industrial complex and giant agri-businesses. They are the entities with unlimited wealth who surround our nation's

Bernie Sanders Revolution

capitol with thousands of well-paid lobbyists, who to a significant degree write the laws that we live under. Today, we have a demagogue in the White House who, for cheap political gain, is attempting to deflect the attention of the American people away from the real crises that we face and, instead, is doing what demagogues always do and that is divide people up and legislate hatred. This is a president who supports brutal family separations, border walls, Muslim bans, anti-LGBT policies, deportations and voter suppression. It is my very strong belief that the United States must reject that path of hatred and divisiveness and instead find the moral conviction to choose a different path, a higher path, a path of compassion, justice and love. It is the path that I call democratic socialism. Over eighty years ago Franklin Delano Roosevelt helped create a government that made transformative progress in protecting the

Bernie Sanders Revolution

needs of working families. Today, in the second decade of the 21st century, we must take up the unfinished business of the New Deal and carry it to completion. This is the unfinished business of the Democratic Party and the vision we must accomplish. In order to accomplish that goal, it means committing ourselves to protecting political rights, to protecting civil rights and to protect economic rights of all people in this country. As FDR stated in his 1944 State of the Union address: "We have come to a clear realization of the fact that true individual freedom cannot exist without economic security and independence." Today, our Bill of Rights guarantees the American people a number of important constitutionally protected political rights. And while we understand that these rights have not always been respected and we have so much more work to do, we are proud that our constitution guarantees freedom of religion, freedom of expression, freedom of

Bernie Sanders Revolution

assembly, a free press and other rights because we understand that we can never have true American freedom unless we are free from authoritarian tyranny. Now, we must take the next step forward and guarantee every man, woman and child in our country basic economic rights the right to quality health care, the right to as much education as one needs to succeed in our society, the right to a good job that pays a living wage, the right to affordable housing, the right to a secure retirement, and the right to live in a clean environment. We must recognize that in the 21st century, in the wealthiest country in the history of the world, economic rights are human rights. That is what I mean by democratic socialism. As Dr. Martin Luther King Jr. said, "Call it democracy, or call it democratic socialism, but there must be a better distribution of wealth within this country for all of God's children." To realize this vision, we must not view America only as a population of

Bernie Sanders Revolution

disconnected individuals, we must also view ourselves as part of "an inescapable network of mutuality, tied in a single garment of destiny," as Dr. King put it. In other words, we are in this together. We must see ourselves as part of one nation, one community and one society regardless of race, gender, religion, sexual orientation, or country of origin. This quintessentially American idea is literally emblazoned on our coins: E Pluribus Unum. From the many, one. And, I should tell you, it is enshrined in the motto of our campaign for the presidency Not me, Us. Let me be clear. I do understand that I and other progressives will face massive attacks from those who attempt to use the word "socialism" as a slur. But I should also tell you that I have faced and overcome these attacks for decades and I am not the only one. Let us remember that in 1932, Republican President Herbert Hoover claimed that Franklin Roosevelt's New Deal was, "a disguise for the

Bernie Sanders Revolution

totalitarian state." In 1936 former Democratic New York Governor and presidential candidate Al Smith said in a speech about FDR's New Deal policies, "Just get the platform of the Democratic Party and get the platform of the Socialist Party and lay them down on your dining-room table, side by side." When President Harry Truman proposed a national health care program, the American Medical Association hired Ronald Reagan as their pitchman. The AMA called the legislation that stemmed from his proposal "socialized medicine" claiming that White House staff were, "followers of the Moscow party line."

In 1960, Ronald Reagan in a letter to Richard Nixon wrote the following about John F. Kennedy: "Under the tousled boyish haircut is still old Karl Marx." In the 1990s, then Congressman Newt Gingrich claimed President Bill Clinton's health care plan was "centralized bureaucratic socialism." The conservative

Bernie Sanders Revolution

Heritage Foundation has claimed that the Children's Health Insurance Program (CHIP) was "a step towards socialism." Former Speaker of the House John Boehner claimed the stimulus package, the omnibus spending bill and the budget proposed by President Barack Obama were "all one big down payment on a new American socialist experiment." In this regard, President Harry Truman was right when he said that: "Socialism is the epithet they have hurled at every advance the people have made in the last 20 years. Socialism is what they called Social Security. Socialism is what they called farm price supports. Socialism is what they called bank deposit insurance. Socialism is what they called the growth of free and independent labor organizations. Socialism is their name for almost anything that helps all the people." Now let's be clear: while President Trump and his fellow oligarchs attack us for our support of democratic socialism, they don't really oppose all forms of socialism. They may hate democratic socialism because it benefits working people, but they absolutely love corporate socialism that enriches Trump and other billionaires.

September 22, 2019 Bernie Sanders Speech
Thank you very much for being out today. And let me thank Mayor Clark for welcoming us to Norman. And let me thank all of you for coming out. This is a great, great turn out. We appreciate it. I think I'm going to be saying a few things here in Oklahoma that you don't usually hear in Oklahoma. But maybe it's time you did hear it in Oklahoma. And let me begin by quoting one of the great leaders of the 20th century, Nelson Mandela. And Nelson Mandela said, "It always seems impossible until it is done." "It always seems impossible until it is done." You all know what that means? What it means is that every day, the establishment and the media and everybody tells you that you can't

Bernie Sanders Revolution

accomplish big things, that you got to think really, really small. And basically, they also tell you that you're powerless. You don't have any power. Why do you want to get involved in the political process? The deck is stacked against working people. You got nothing. Go home. Go to sleep. Forget about it. They will continue to control this country and the world. Well, I'm here to tell you something different. I'm here to tell you that you have enormous power if you are prepared to use that power. Because at the end of the day, the 1% has unlimited amounts of money, has enormous control over the media. They control the economy. But at the end of the day, the 1% is 1%. And we are 99%. And I don't have a PhD in mathematics, but I do know that 99% is a hell of a bigger number than 1%.: And the other thing that I want to say, and I say this to the young people, people like myself. We young people. And what I want to say to you very sincerely is that you are the most

Bernie Sanders Revolution

progressive generation, young generation in the history of this country. You are a generation that has fought against racism. You have a fought against sexism. You have for against homophobia. You have fought against Xenophobia. And you have fought against religious bigotry. All of the things that Donald Trump is supporting. But while your generation is the most progressive young generation probably in American history, the bad news is you do not vote in the kind of numbers you should be voting in. And I know that a lot of your friends when they ask you what you did this afternoon, you said you went to a Bernie Sanders rally. They'll kind of look at you quizzically and they said, "Why would you possibly do that?" That's right. And you look them in the eye and you say you here because you're sick and tired of people complaining about low wages. You're sick and tired about people complaining about the high cost of

Bernie Sanders Revolution

college and college debt. You're tired of people talking about climate change. You are prepared, and you want them to be prepared to have the courage to stand up to powerful special interest and make the kinds of changes this country desperately needs. You all know who Woody Guthrie is. All right. Woody Guthrie is one of the great song writers in recent history, born here in Oklahoma. And he said something. He wrote a song which basically said, "Which side are you on?" And what he was talking about is, "Are you on the side of working people were struggling for dignity, or are you on the side of the wealthy and the powerful?" And we are here to say to Woody, "Woody, we are on the side of the working class of this country." And let me be very blunt with you and tell you what politicians don't tell you because I think every now and then it's important that we tell the truth, every now and then. I don't want to overstate it. And here is the truth, the truth you're not going to

Bernie Sanders Revolution

see on television, you're not going to hear in the radio, you're not going to hear in the United States Congress. And that you live in a political system today that is corrupt. It is corrupt because you have billionaires who have unlimited amounts of money, contributing hundreds of millions of dollars, hundreds of millions of dollars to the candidates who represent their greedy interests. So the system is about that you get one vote, and that's great, and you get a vote and that's great. But they got the money and they will buy the ads on television, they will give massive amounts of campaign, contributions they will thought Super PACS. That is a corrupt political system. We have people who fought and died for American democracy and as president I intend to make sure that we have a real democracy one person, one vote. And we're going to end this disastrous Citizen's United, Supreme Court decision, we're gonna move to public funding of elections. And I

Bernie Sanders Revolution

want all of you. And I mean this very seriously. I
want you to be thinking about running for office.
You can do it. Whether it's school board
whether it's city council whatever it may be, you
can do it. Listen I am a member of the United
States Senate. And if you think you don't know
enough for to run for local office, trust me I know
the United States Senate. You do know enough.
But you got to the confidence. You can't allow
people to intimidate you, not whether you're
running for office or anything else. If you got the
heart if you got respect for other people, if you
believe in justice, stand up and struggle with us
and give some thought to running for office.
Now, four years ago. I want to tell you how
change takes place. Change never takes place
from the top on down, you all know that. Change
always takes place from the bottom on up, study
your history, that is the history of the labor
movement. It is the history of the Civil Rights
Movement. It is the history of the Women's

Bernie Sanders Revolution

Movement, it is the history of the gay movement, it is the history of the environmental movement, and all of you know that as part of that change, people all over the world, not just in the United States all over the world took to the streets a few days ago saying they demand action, for climate change It's right, right? Okay we're going to get to that in one minute. But here is how change always takes place, see politicians and the ruling elite they dont want you to be involved in anything because things are going pretty good, right now. Richer getting much, richer. We have a massive level of income and wealth inequality. And I want you all to hear this, because it's not talked about in Congress, it's not talked about in the media, you got three people in America who own more wealth than the bottom half of American people. We need a little bit of outrage on that. You got the top one percent owning more wealth than the bottom 92% here in Oklahoma and in

Bernie Sanders Revolution

Vermont and all over this country. You've got people working two or three jobs trying to feed their families at inadequate wages and 49% 49% of all new income goes to the top one present. Now, the big money interest in this country don't want us to discuss income and wealth inequality. We will not only discuss income and wealth inequality, but when I am president, we're going to deal with income and wealth inequality. Trump and his friends gave over a trillion dollars in tax breaks to the 1%, and large profitable corporations. You have the absurd situation that today companies like Amazon, anybody know how much Amazon paid in taxes, last year? That's right. See you got a company and make 10 billion bucks paid zero in profits trust me we're going to end that absurdity when we are in the White House. Tell you what else we're going to do, we're going to make it clear that starvation wages in America are not acceptable four years ago

Bernie Sanders Revolution

when I came here, I said that if you work 40 hours a week, you shouldn't be living in poverty. We've got to raise that minimal wage to at least 15 bucks an hour. And people said Bernie, you're crazy, your extreme can't be done. In the last four years, seven states and the United States Congress have raised the minimum wage to 15 bucks an hour. If the people want it to be done and they do it will be done, and together we're going to raise the minimum wage in this country to a living wage, 15 bucks an hour. And we are also going to establish equal pay for equal work. We're going to end the absurdity of women making 80 cents on the dollar compared to men. And we are going to make it easier for workers to join unions that's what we're going to do. And there's another issue I talked about four years ago, whatever they'll say Bernie, you're crazy. Can't be done. What I said is "Look in the wealthiest country in the history of the world. We've got to rethink

Bernie Sanders Revolution

what free public education is about. It's no longer good enough to go from K through 12 We've got to make public colleges and universities tuition free. And all over this country people started saying. "Yeah, that makes sense". Why does Germany have free college education why does Scandinavia? How are our young people going to go out and get the jobs that they need and make it into the middle class unless they have a good education, and why don't we make sure that everybody has that opportunity regardless of the income of their families. And you know what's happened over the last four years? State after state, county after county is moving in that direction. In fact, just the other day state of New Mexico, said they will make their public colleges and universities tuition free. Point is that when you stand up and fight for something, when you make the give the establishment and offer they cannot refuse when you demand justice,

Bernie Sanders Revolution

whether it's education or the economy or whatever, you will win. And our job now is to make public colleges and universities tuition free and free expand Pell Grants and work study programs so that every person in this country, regardless of income has the opportunity to go to college or to a trade school they want so they can make it into the middle class. And I'll tell you what else we're going to do. We're going to cancel all student debt in America. Question, question, How many of you are dealing with students that are worried about... There you go alright. So here is what I want you to think about, Okay, this is what this is what I want you to think about. Get it in your heads.11 years ago against my vote, the United States Congress bailed out the crooks on Wall Street who destroyed our economy. They gave them 700 billion out of the treasury and trillions of dollars of zero-interest loans. They sure are couple of years ago Trump and his friends gave over a trillion dollars in tax breaks to the 1% and large corporations. So what I want you to think about and to understand if we can give tax breaks to billionaires if we can be out the crooks on Wall Street we most certainly can cancel all student debt. And we pay for that. We pay for that through a tax a modest tax, I would say on Wall Street speculation. We bailed them out, 11 years ago. It is their time to help the working people of this country today. And let me say a word on an issue that I've been working on for many, many years and I think we're going to have some major success. I want you all to know that the United States of America is the only major country on Earth, not to guarantee healthcare to all people as a human right. And together we're going to end that absurdity. Right now as a nation we are spending twice as much per person on healthcare as do the people of any other industrialized nation, about $11,000 a year per person. And yet for all of that money

Bernie Sanders Revolution

this is what you get: 87 million uninsured or under-insured, 30,000 Americans dying every single year because they don't get to a doctor when they should, and you're looking at 500,000 people a year going bankrupt because of medical bills. Can you imagine the vulgarity of a system in which people go bankrupt for what? They came down with cancer or heart disease. We are going to end that cruelty. Last year, the healthcare industry made a $100 billion in profit. And we are going to create a healthcare system which provides quality care for all, not 100 billion in profits for the healthcare industry. And I want all of you to know we are going to take on the greed and the price fixing of the pharmaceutical industry. This is an industry that is ripping off the American people, charging us by far the highest prices in the world. One out of five Americans cannot afford to fill the prescriptions their doctors prescribe. That is absurd. Under our Medicare for all program not only will everybody

Bernie Sanders Revolution

have freedom of choice with regard to the doctor, hospital you want to go to, but nobody in America will pay more than $200 a year for the prescription drugs that they need. And let me say a word on another issue of enormous consequence. And yes I do know I am in Oklahoma but we got to deal with this issue. And that is we have a president who thinks that climate change is a hoax. Well, I happen to believe that Donald Trump is a hoax. And I think, I think we need a president who actually believes in science. But the scientists are telling us, is not only that climate change is real, not only it is already causing devastating problems in our country and around the world...

What I was saying is that climate change is very, very real. And what we are seeing now all over the world, as you know, are rising sea levels, you're seeing incredible floods. We're seeing it right in front of our eyes. You all see what's going on in Texas, unprecedented rain.

Bernie Sanders Revolution

You saw what happened in Bahamas, an incredible extreme weather disturbance, unprecedented storm velocities. You saw what happened to Puerto Rico a couple of years ago. Right now there's forest fires raging in Bolivia, heat waves this summer in Europe, India, Pakistan, Brazil. We're seeing a global crisis and here is what the scientists are telling us. The scientists are telling us that we have 11 years in order to get our act together to make certain that there are not irreparable damages done to our planet, damages that cannot be repaired. So we are facing a global crisis. And I am very proud to tell you, I really am, that I have listened to the scientists and we have introduced a climate change plan which is the boldest plan ever introduced by any presidential candidate in the history of this country. And I want to say to the workers in the fossil fuel industry I am perhaps the most, the strongest pro-worker member of the United States

Bernie Sanders Revolution

Congress I have 100% lifetime voting record for unions and for workers. So I am not against the workers in the oil industry or in the coal industry or the gas industry. I am against and will combat climate change. And what we have built in to our plan, which is a very expansive plan among many other things, we have put in hundreds of billions of dollars to protect those workers in the fossil fuel industry who might lose their jobs. And I'm talking about the most generous protections ever offered. We're talking about five years of salary, we're talking about health care, we're talking about job training. So I want to say to those workers, we understand that you're working hard to put food on the table for your families, you are not our enemy. But together we must come to grips with the global crisis of climate change. And the other thing that I want to say is, as you all know, climate change is not an American issue, it is a global issue. We can't do it alone. If we did everything magically

Bernie Sanders Revolution

tomorrow it still wouldn't matter enough because we need the entire planet to work together. So here is my dream and what I will attempt to accomplish as President of the United States, and that is to tell the world in this unprecedentedly dangerous moment that instead of spending a trillion and a half dollars on weapons of destruction designed to kill each other how about pooling our resources and combating our common enemy, which is climate change. And I want to say a word about something that is, I feel very passionate about and that is the need to reform a broken and racist criminal justice system. So how do I look in this hat? You like it? I wonder what... I'm asking should I wear it in Texas? Okay. But we got a criminal justice system. And I want you to just to think about this again. Think outside of the box. We have more people in jail than any other country on Earth. You all know that? We've got over two million people in jail

Bernie Sanders Revolution

disproportionately African-American, Latino and Native American. My job as President of the United States will be to invest in our young people, in jobs and education, not build more jails and have more incarceration. We under our Criminal Justice Plan will end all private prisons and detention centers in America. And we're also going to end the so-called War on Drugs. Now, let me ask you one question, I've been asking this kind of question around the country. I've been amazed by the answers I got, I don't know really how it is in Oklahoma, but here's my question. How many of you know somebody who has been arrested for possession of marijuana? Wow that's unbelievable, and that is the kind of response we're hearing all over the country. Now the good news is, four years ago, I talked about the need to legalize marijuana. And because of the ethics of people all over this country, you know what's happening, state after state is moving to either decriminalize or

Bernie Sanders Revolution

legalize Marijuana. And I want to take it a step further because many people who were arrested for possession of marijuana, they have criminal records and sometimes those records prevent them from getting the jobs or the other opportunities they should be getting. And that is why we're going to expunge the records of anybody arrested for marijuana. There's another issue that we have got to address. We got a president, and I say this with no joy in my heart, a president who is a racist and a sexist and a xenophobe and a homophobe and a religious bigot, that's what he is. And he thinks he is going to win re-election, this is his plan, it is not complicated. He thinks he's going to win re-election by dividing the American people up based on the color of our skin, based on where we were born or our religion or whatever. Well, Mr. Trump we got some bad news for you that ain't going to happen. And in terms of immigration, we are going to stop the racism and the demonization of undocumented people. We are going to pass comprehensive immigration reform and a path towards citizenship. On my first day in office through executive order, we are gonna restore legal status to the 1.8 million young people in the DACA program. And we are going to develop a humane border policy which does not snatch babies from the arms of their mothers. Yesterday I was in Iowa and I talked to a woman and she told me she is from El Salvador. And she told me that when she was under detention she was pregnant, I think eight months pregnant, she was put in a room with 15 other pregnant women and it was so crowded that women had to take turns lying on the ground in order to sleep. That is not the way you treat a pregnant woman, that is not the way you treat any human being. So we will develop an immigration system that is non-racist and one that we are proud of. And let me say a couple of other issues that might be a little bit sensitive here in Oklahoma. And that is... I am horrified and I know that many of you are horrified when we turn on the TV, and we hear about another mass shooting. And we are pained to know that millions of children go to school and they are frightened, they are frightened of what may happen when they're in school. How awful is that? Now, what the American people want and that is true, that is true in rural areas, like Vermont and I suspect Oklahoma, and it is true in urban areas and what the American people want is common sense gun safety legislation. So let me just tell you that this president will not be intimidated by the NRA. We will do what the American people want, expand background checks, end the gun show loophole. Make it impossible for people to legally buy guns and then sell them to criminals, and we will ban the sale and distribution of assault weapons in this country. And let me say something to the men in

Bernie Sanders Revolution

the audience. And that is right now, all over this country, there is a massive attack against women's rights. In state after state, there are efforts to take away what I believe is a woman's constitutional right to control her own body. And today I am asking the men, stand with the women. It is a woman and not the government who has the right to make those most personal decisions. Let me conclude by just saying this. This is an unprecedented moment in American history because we have a president who in my view is the most dangerous president in the modern history of this country. He is a president who is a pathological liar, who does not respect the Constitution. And I think as we are already seeing and we will see more of, he will merge government agencies with his campaign in order to try to win. But on top of Trump, we have crisis after crisis after crisis. And what this campaign's message is about, it's called us not me because I understand that no president, not Bernie

Bernie Sanders Revolution

Sanders or anybody else, can do it alone. The only way we stand up to the greed and corruption of the corporate elite, and I'm talking about Wall Street, I'm talking about the insurance companies and the drug companies and the fossil fuel industry. I'm talking about the military industrial complex and the prison industrial complex. I'm talking about the whole damn 1%. So what our campaign is about and it is unique, it is unique now, and is maybe unique in American history. I'm asking for your help not only to win the Oklahoma primary. I'm asking, not only for your help to win the Democratic nomination. I'm here asking not only for your help to defeat Donald Trump. What I am asking from you also, this is hard stuff, it ain't easy stuff, but the future of the country and the planet depends upon it. I am asking your help to work with me to transform this country, to transform our economy and create a government that works for all of us not just the 1%. It ain't Bernie it's you. I know what my job is as a candidate, I know what my job will be as president, but I cannot accomplish the things that need to be accomplished unless you and millions of other people are prepared to stand up for economic justice, for social justice, for racial justice, for environmental justice. So today I am here to ask you to join the justice campaign. Let's stand up. Let's fight back. Let's transform this country. Thank you all very much.

March 4th 2020 Bernie Sanders Speech

We're campaigning and doing everything we can to win in Michigan and Washington, Mississippi, North Dakota, Idaho and Missouri. What this campaign I think is increasingly about is which side are you on? Our campaign is unprecedented because there has never been a campaign in recent history that has taken on the entire corporate establishment. And I'm talking about Wall Street and I'm talking about the insurance companies and the drug companies and the fossil fuel industry. There has been never a campaign in recent history which has taken on the entire political establishment and that is an establishment which is working frantically to try to defeat us and there's not been a campaign I think that it has been having to deal with the kind of venom we're seeing from some in the corporate media. This campaign has been compared to the Corona virus on television. We have been described as the Nazi army marching across France, et cetera, et cetera. As we come into the last several months of this campaign, what I hope very much is that what we can focus on is an issue oriented campaign which deals with the concerns of the American people. As some of you may recall, the last debate that took place really was I think insulting to the American people. It was a food fight. It was about who could yell the loudest. That's not what the American people want. They

Bernie Sanders Revolution

want a serious debate on serious issues. Joe Biden, is somebody I have known for many years, I like Joe. I think he is a very decent human being. Joe and I have a very different voting record. Joe and I have a very different vision for the future of this country and Joe and I are running very different campaigns. And my hope is that in the coming months we will be able to debate and discuss the very significant differences that we have. Joe is running a campaign which is obviously heavily supported by the corporate establishment. At last count has received funding from at least 60 billionaires, 60 billionaires. Our campaign has received more campaign contributions from more Americans averaging $18.50 than any campaign in the history of our country at this point in time. So what does it mean when you have a campaign which is funded very significantly by the wealthy and the powerful? Does anyone seriously believe that a president backed by the corporate world is going to bring about the changes in this country that working families and the middle class and lower income people desperately need? We are going to the Midwest. I'll be in Michigan shortly and as I think everybody knows, Michigan, Wisconsin, Indiana, Midwest in general, Minnesota have been very hard hit by disastrous trade agreements. And Joe is going to have to explain to the people and the union workers in the Midwest why he supported disastrous trade agreements like NAFTA and PNTR with China which have cost this country millions of good paying jobs and in fact have resulted in a race to the bottom where people are now earning lower wages. Millions of people today lost good paying jobs in manufacturing and are now earning substantially less than they used to. Joe is going to have to explain to the American people why he voted for a Wall Street bailout, something that I vigorously opposed. Joe is going to have to explain to the American people who are so tired of endless wars which have cost us too many lives, destabilized many regions around the world, have cost us trillions of dollars, why he was a leader in getting us involved in the war in Iraq at a time when half of our people are living paycheck to paycheck and struggling to make ends meet. Joe is going to have to explain to the American people why he voted for a disastrous bankruptcy bill, which benefited the credit card companies. Joe is going to have to explain to people all over this country why he was on the floor of the Senate time and time again, talking about the need not only to cut social security, but Medicare, Medicaid and veterans programs. How does that happen? Why would a Democrat talk about cutting social security, Medicare, Medicaid, and veterans programs? Joe and I have a very different opinion with regarding healthcare. Joe essentially wants to maintain what I consider to

Bernie Sanders Revolution

be a dysfunctional and cruel healthcare system in which we are spending twice as much per person on healthcare as are the people of any other country and yet we have 87 million Americans who are uninsured, underinsured. 30,000 people who are dying and 500,000 people will go bankrupt every single year because of medically related bills and on top of that, we pay by far not even close, highest prices in the world for prescription drugs from an industry which is involved in collusion and price fixing. So the American people have got to understand that this is a conflict about ideas, about a record, about a vision for where we go forward. And I like Joe. Joe is a decent guy and I do not want this campaign to degenerate into a Trump type effort where we're attacking each other, where it's personal attacks. That is the last thing this country wants. Joe has his ideas, his record, his vision for the future. I have mine and I look forward to a serious debate on the

Bernie Sanders Revolution

serious issues facing this country. Yeah, and I would hope that the media will help us do that. Allow that kind of debate to take place. And by the way, I would offer Joe, because I know the issue of healthcare among many other issues, is such an enormously important issue, I would hope that instead of having a debate where we have to spend 28 seconds trying to respond to a complicated issue, maybe we can spend an hour talking about why the United States is the only major country on earth not to guarantee healthcare to all people through something like a Medicare for all single payer program."

March 8th 2020 Bernie Sanders Speech

Thank you all very much for being here tonight and thank you for being part of a political revolution which will transform America. Thank you for being part of a campaign which is not only going to win the Democratic nomination, which is not only going to defeat

Bernie Sanders Revolution

Donald Trump, the most dangerous president in modern American history, but with your help is going to transform this country and, finally, create an economy and government which works for all Americans, and not just the one percent. Today, I want to welcome you to a campaign which says, loudly and clearly, that the underlying principles of our government will not be greed, kleptocracy, hatred and lies. It will not be racism, sexism, xenophobia, homophobia and religious bigotry. All of that is going to end. The principles of our government will be based on justice: economic justice, social justice, racial justice and environmental justice. Tonight, I want to welcome you to a campaign which tells the powerful special interests who control so much of our economic and political life that we will no longer tolerate the greed of Wall Street, corporate America and the billionaire class greed which has resulted in this country having more income and wealth inequality than any

Bernie Sanders Revolution

other major country on earth. No we will no longer stand idly by and allow 3 people in this country to own more wealth than the bottom half of America while, at the same time, nearly 20 percent of our children live in poverty, veterans sleep out on the streets and seniors cannot afford their prescription drugs. We will no longer accept 46 percent of all new income going to the top 1 percent, while millions of Americans are forced to work 2 or 3 jobs just to survive and over half of our people live paycheck to paycheck, frightened to death about what happens to them financially if their car breaks down or their child becomes sick. Together, we are going to create a political system which is based on the democratic principles of one person - one vote - and end a corrupt system which allows billionaires to buy elections. Yes. We are going to overturn Citizens United and move to public funding of elections. Today, we fight for a political revolution. And tonight, I want

Bernie Sanders Revolution

to offer a very special thanks to the people of the great state of Iowa. In 2016, this is where the political revolution began. Thank you Iowa. When I first came here to campaign in 2015 not a whole lot of people knew who I was, nobody took our campaign seriously, and we were at 3 percent in the polls. Further, the ideas that we were talking about then were considered by establishment politicians and mainstream media to be "radical" and "extreme" ideas, they said, that nobody in America would support.

Raising the minimum wage to a living wage. Too radical. Guaranteeing health care to all as a right, not a privilege. Too radical. Creating up to 15 million jobs by rebuilding our crumbling infrastructure with a one trillion dollar investment. Too radical. Aggressively combatting climate change. Too radical. Reforming our broken criminal justice and immigration systems. Too radical. Not taking money from super PACs and the rich. Too

Bernie Sanders Revolution

radical. Ending the power of super delegates at the Democratic Convention. Too radical. Well, a funny thing happened in Iowa over that year. On Caucus Night we didn't win 3% of the vote, we won 50% of the vote and half of the pledged delegates. And that great start in Iowa led us to win victories in 22 states around the country, 13 million votes, over 1700 delegates at the convention and more votes from young people Black, White, Latino, Asian American and Native American, than Trump and Clinton combined. And by the way. Those ideas that we talked about 4 years ago that seemed so very radical at that time. Well, today, virtually all of those ideas are supported by a majority of the American people and have overwhelming support from Democrats and independents - and they're ideas that Democratic candidates for president to school board are now supporting. So Iowa, you helped begin the political revolution in 2016 and, with your help on this

Bernie Sanders Revolution

campaign, we are going to complete what we started here. We're going to turn our vision and our progressive agenda into reality. Today, as we launch our campaign here in Iowa, we say to the private health insurance companies, whether you like it or not, the United States will join every other major country on earth and guarantee healthcare to all people as a right. All Americans are entitled to go to the doctor when they're sick and not go bankrupt after staying in the hospital. We will no longer accept the absurdity of paying almost twice as much per capita on health care, while we have a lower life expectancy and worse health care outcomes than many other countries. The goal of health care must be to provide quality care to all in a cost effective way, not tens of billions in profits for the insurance companies and outrageous compensation packages for CEOs. In 2017, the top 65 healthcare CEO's made $1.7 billion in compensation including: $83.2 million to David

Bernie Sanders Revolution

Wichmann, the CEO of UnitedHealth Group and 58.7 million to Mark Bertolini, the CEO of Aetna. We need a health care system that invests in disease prevention, doctors, nurses, dentists and rural clinics. We don't a system which makes insurance companies and their CEOs super rich. Yes. We will pass a Medicare for all single-payer program. Health care is a right. And, by the way, our legislation improves health care for seniors by providing coverage for dental care, hearing aids and eye glasses. Today, we say to the pharmaceutical industry, that you will no longer charge the American people the highest prices in the world for prescription drugs, the result being that one out of five Americans cannot afford the prescriptions their doctors prescribe. Seniors in this country should not have to cut their pills in half. The outrageous greed of the pharmaceutical industry is going to end. We are going to lower prescription drug prices in this country. Today, we say to

Bernie Sanders Revolution

Walmart, the fast food industry and other low wage employers: Stop paying your employees starvation wages.. Yes. We are going to raise the federal minimum wage to a living wage $15 an hour. Nobody who works 40 hours a week in this country should live in poverty. And yes. We're going to make it easier for people to join unions, not harder. Four years ago, when we talked about the idea of a $15 an hour minimum wage, it seemed like an impossible dream. Well, since then, I'm happy to tell you that 5 states have passed $15 an hour legislation and, just yesterday, the U.S. House Committee on Labor and Education reported out a bill that will raise the federal minimum wage from $7.25 an hour to $15 an hour. And, I believe, that bill will pass the full House within the month. And, by the way. Today we say to corporate America that artificial intelligence and robotics are not going to be used just to throw workers out on the street. This exploding technology must serve human needs, not just corporate profits. Today we say to the American people that we will rebuild our crumbling infrastructure: our roads, our bridges, our rail system and subways, our airports, our water systems and wastewater plants - and when we do that we create up to 13 million good paying jobs. And let's be clear. When I talk about infrastructure and clean water we're talking about strengthening clean water laws so that corporate polluters stop poisoning the drinking water that communities in Iowa and across the country rely on. Today we say to the parents in this country that you and your kids deserve quality, affordable childcare. The children are our future, and they deserve the best possible head start in life with a high quality, universal pre-K program. Today, we say to our young people that we want you to get the best education that you can, regardless of the income of your family. Good jobs require a good education. That is why we are going to make

Bernie Sanders Revolution

public colleges and universities tuition free, and substantially lower the outrageous level of student debt that currently exists. America once had the best educated workforce in the world, and we are going to make that happen again. Today, we say to our senior citizens, that we understand that you cannot live in dignity when you are trying to survive on $13,000 or $14,000 a year in Social Security benefits. My Republican colleagues want to cut Social Security but we have some bad news for them. We're not going to cut Social Security benefits. We're going to expand them. Today, we say to Donald Trump and the fossil fuel industry that climate change is not a hoax but is an existential threat to our country and the entire planet - and we intend to transform our energy system away from fossil fuel and into energy efficiency and sustainable energy and, in the process, create millions of good paying jobs. All of us have a moral responsibility to make certain that the

Bernie Sanders Revolution

planet we leave to our children and grandchildren is healthy and habitable. Today, we say to the prison-industrial-complex that we are going to bring about real criminal justice reform. We are going to end the international embarrassment of having more people in jail than any other country on earth. Instead of spending $80 billion a year on jails and incarceration, we are going to invest in jobs and education for our young people. No more private prisons and detention centers. No more profiteering from locking people up. No more "war on drugs." No more keeping people in jail because they're too poor to afford cash bail. And by the way, when we talk about criminal justice reform, we're going to change a system in which tens of thousands of Americans every year get criminal records for possessing marijuana, but not one major Wall Street executive went to jail for destroying our economy in 2008 as a result of their greed, recklessness and illegal behavior. No. They didn't go to jail. They got a trillion-dollar bailout. Today, we say to the American people that instead of demonizing the undocumented immigrants in this country, we're going to pass comprehensive immigration reform and provide a path toward citizenship. We're going to provide legal status to the 1.8 million young people eligible for the DACA program, and develop a humane border policy for those who seek asylum. No more snatching babies from the arms of their mothers. Today, we say to the top 1 percent and the large profitable corporations in this country - people who have never had it so good that under a Bernie Sanders administration we're going to end the massive tax breaks and loopholes that you currently enjoy. We will no longer accept the absurd situation where large corporations like Amazon, Netflix and General Motors pay nothing in federal income taxes after raking in

Bernie Sanders Revolution

billions in profits. We will no longer tolerate the situation in which the wealthy and large corporations stash billions in tax havens throughout the world. Yes the wealthy and multi-national corporations in this country will start paying their fair share of taxes. We are going to end austerity for working families, and provide some austerity for large, multi-national corporations. Today we say to the military-industrial-complex that we will not continue to spend $700 billion a year on the military more than the next ten nations combined. We're going to invest in affordable housing, we're going to invest in public education, we're going to invest in rebuilding our crumbling infrastructure not more nuclear weapons and never-ending wars. Brothers and sisters: We're going to win this election not because we have a super PAC funded by billionaires. We're going to win this election because we will put together the strongest grassroots coalition in the history of

Bernie Sanders Revolution

American politics. Donald Trump wants to divide us up by the color of our skin, our country of origin, our gender, our religion and our sexual orientation. We are going to do exactly the opposite. We are going to bring our people together – black, white, Latino, Native American, Asian American, gay and straight, young and old, men and women, native born and immigrant. We are going to bring our people together for an unprecedented grassroots effort, which, I am happy to tell you, already has over one million people signed up as volunteers. Brothers and sisters: As someone who represents Vermont, one of the most rural states in the country, let me be very honest with you in saying that the U.S. Congress has, for too long, ignored the many crises facing rural America. In Iowa, in Vermont and all over this country, we have seen more and more young people leave the small towns they grew up in and love, not because they don't want to stay, but because

Bernie Sanders Revolution

there are fewer and fewer jobs that pay a living wage. We have seen schools, churches and community centers shut down, and once vibrant Main Streets become boarded up and deserted. In Vermont, Iowa and all across rural America, we have seen family farmers go out of business as the prices they receive for their products decline rapidly and large agri-business corporations and factory farming take over agriculture. We have seen rural hospitals and nursing homes shut down, and not enough doctors to provide the quality health care that rural American deserves. Tragically, instead of seeing good jobs, education and health care coming into our rural communities, we are far too often seeing despair and depression and a terrible increase in suicide and opioid addiction. Brothers and sisters. We need policies for rural America that represent the needs of working people and farmers, not agri-business and multi-national corporations. Among many other things that need to be done is for the federal government to enforce anti-trust laws, and I will appoint an Attorney General who will do just that. It is not acceptable to me that the top four packing companies control more than 80 percent of the beef market, 63 percent of the pork market, and 53 percent of the chicken market. And these numbers understate the situation. In many communities, there really is only one buyer, which means food producers are at their mercy. They must use that corporation's feed and livestock, they must accept that corporation's costs, and they must accept that corporation's lower and lower payment rates. In many cases, the farmer doesn't even own the livestock or supplies -- they are effectively contract employees who are forced to lease everything, and then get paid an inadequate wage for their very hard work. With the federal government not enforcing antitrust laws, we have seen mergers like the Bayer-

Bernie Sanders Revolution

Monsanto approved, giving the two largest conglomerates 78 percent of the corn seed market. Further, instead of protecting family owned farms, federal support for agriculture is skewed toward huge farms. The top 10 percent of farms currently receive 77 percent of all subsidies. The time is long overdue for the U.S. government to stand with rural America, and that is exactly what I do. Brothers and sisters. Over the last two years, and before, you and I and millions of Americans have stood up and fought for justice in every part of our society. And we've had some successes. Together, as billionaires and large corporations have attacked unions, destroyed pensions, deregulated the banks, and slashed wages, we have succeeded in raising the minimum wage to $15 in states and cities across the country. And forced large corporations like Amazon and Disney to do the same. And we have supported teachers who successfully stood up for their kids in strike after

Bernie Sanders Revolution

strike after strike. Together, as the forces of militarism have kept us engaged in unending wars, we have stood arm in arm to fight back. For the first time in 45 years, we have utilized the War Powers Act to move us forward in ending the horrific Saudi-led war in Yemen. Together, as so many of our young people have received criminal records for nonviolent offenses, we have fought to end the war on drugs, and have seen state after state decriminalize marijuana, and have seen communities expunge the criminal records of those arrested on these charges. Let's be honest: while we have won some victories, our struggles have not always been successful. But I am here to tell you, that because of all the work we have done, we are now on the brink of winning not just an election, but transforming our country. And let me tell you what that means. When We are in the White House, we will enact a federal jobs guarantee, to ensure

Bernie Sanders Revolution

that everyone is guaranteed a stable job. There is more than enough work to be done in this country. Let's do it. When We are in the White House we will not only end the decline of rural America, but attack the problem of urban gentrification and build the affordable housing we desperately need all across this country. When We are in the White House, we will move aggressively to end the epidemic of gun violence in this country and pass the common sense gun safety legislation that the overwhelming majority of Americans want. People who should not have guns, will not have guns. When We are in the White House, we are going to address not only the disparities of wealth and income that exist overall in our nation, but we will address the racial disparities of wealth and income. We are going to root out institutional racism wherever it exists. Not only will we end voter suppression, we are going to make it easier for people to vote not harder.

Bernie Sanders Revolution

When We are in the White House, we are going to protect a woman's right to control her own body. That is her decision, not the government's. Make no mistake about it, this struggle is not just about defeating Donald Trump. This struggle is about taking on the incredibly powerful institutions that control the economic and political life of this country. And I'm talking about Wall Street, the insurance companies, the drug companies, the military-industrial complex, agri-business, the prison-industrial complex, the fossil fuel industry and a corrupt campaign finance system that enables billionaires to buy elections. These powerful special interests are going to spend a lot of money to try to defeat us. But we have something they don't have: the power of the people. Brothers and sisters: We have an enormous amount of work in front of us. But this what I believe. If we stand together, if we don't allow Trump and his friends to divide us up; If we stand together as black and white, Latino, Asian American and Native American. If we stand together as gay and straight, men and women, native born and immigrant. If we stand together as rural and urban - north, south, east and west. If we understand that there really is no such thing as blue state or red state, but states throughout the country where working people are struggling to survive. If we stand together, this country has an extraordinary future. Let's make it happen."

March 11th 2020 Bernie Sanders Speech

"Thank you all very much for being here. Let me begin by reiterating what I have said from Day 1 of this campaign, and that is that Donald Trump is the most dangerous president in the modern history of our country and he must be defeated. Tragically, we have a president today who is a pathological liar and who is running a corrupt administration. He clearly does not understand

Bernie Sanders Revolution

the Constitution of the United States and thinks
that he is a president who is above the law. In
my view, he is a racist, a sexist, a homophobe,
a xenophobe and a religious bigot, and he must
be defeated, and I will do everything in my
power to make that happen. Last night,
obviously, was not a good night for our
campaign from a delegate point of view. We lost
in the largest state up for grabs yesterday, the
state of Michigan. We lost
in Mississippi, Missouri, and Idaho.
On the other hand, we won in North Dakota and
we lead the vote count in the state
of Washington, the second-largest state
contested yesterday. With 67 percent of the
votes having been counted, we are a few
thousand votes on top. What became even
more apparent yesterday is that while we are
currently losing the delegate count,
approximately 800 delegates for Joe Biden and
660 for us, we are strongly winning in two

Bernie Sanders Revolution

enormously important areas which will determine the future of our country.

Poll after poll, including exit polls, show that a strong majority of the American people support our progressive agenda. The American people are deeply concerned about the grotesque level of income and wealth inequality in this country, and the American people want the wealthy and large, profitable corporations to start paying their fair share of taxes. Overwhelming support for that. The American people understand that the federal minimum wage of $7.25 an hour is a starvation wage. They want to raise the minimum wage in this country to a living wage of at least $15 an hour. And the American people understand that if our kids are going to make it into the middle class of this country, we must make public colleges and universities and trade schools tuition-free. The American people understand that we cannot continue a cruel and dysfunctional health care system. And it is amazing to me to see that even in conservative states like Mississippi, there is an overwhelming understanding that we are now spending twice as much per capita on health care as do the people of any other country, while 87 million of us remain uninsured or underinsured. And this crisis, this absurd health care system, is becoming more and more obvious to the American people as we face the challenge of a coronavirus pandemic that we are currently experiencing. Imagine facing a pandemic and having 87 million people who are having a difficult time going to a doctor when they need. And the American people know, unlike Donald Trump, that climate change is an existential threat to our country and the planet and that we need to transform our energy system away from fossil fuel to energy efficiency and sustainable energy. And the American people also know that we need fundamental transformation of a broken and racist criminal justice system as well as a cruel immigration system that keeps millions of people living in fear.

But it is not just the ideological debate that our progressive movement is winning. We are winning the generational debate. While Joe Biden continues to do very well with older Americans, especially those people over 65, our campaign continues to win the vast majority of the votes of younger people. And I am talking about people not just in their 20s, but in their 30s and their 40s, the younger generations of this country continue in very strong numbers to support our campaign. Today, I say to the Democratic establishment, in order to win in the future, you need to win the voters who represent the future of our country, and you must speak to the issues of concern to them. You cannot simply be satisfied by winning the votes of people who are older. While our campaign has won the ideological debate, we are losing the debate over electability. I cannot tell you how

Bernie Sanders Revolution

many people our campaign has spoken to who have said and I quote "I like what your campaign stands for. I agree with what your campaign stands for. But I'm going to vote for Joe Biden because I think Joe is the best candidate to defeat Donald Trump." End of quote. We have heard that statement all over this country. Needless to say, I strongly disagree with that assertion, but that is what millions of Democrats and Independents today believe. On Sunday, I very much look forward to the debate in Arizona with my friend, Joe Biden. And let me be very frank as to the questions that I will be asking Joe. Joe, what are you going to do for the 500,000 people who will go bankrupt in our country because of medically related debt? And what are you going to do for the working people of this country and small businesspeople who are paying on average 20 percent of their incomes for health care? Joe, what are you going to do to end the absurdity of the United

Bernie Sanders Revolution

States of America being the only major country on earth where health care is not a human right? Are you really going to veto a Medicare for all bill, if it is passed in Congress? Joe, how are you going to respond to the scientists who tell us we have seven or eight years remaining to transform our energy system before irreparable harm takes place to this planet because of the ravages of climate change? Joe, at a time when most young people need a higher education to make it into the middle class, what are you going to do to make sure that all of our people can go to college or trade school, regardless of their income? And what are you going to do about the millions of people who are struggling with outrageous levels of student debt? Joe, at a time when we have more people in jail than communist China, a nation four times our size, what are you going to do to end mass incarceration and a racist criminal justice system? And what are you going

Bernie Sanders Revolution

to do to end the terror that millions of undocumented people experience right now because of our broken and inhumane immigration system? Joe, what are you going to do about the fact that we have the highest rate of childhood poverty of almost any major country on Earth and are living with the fact that 500,000 people tonight are homeless and 18 million families are spending half of their income to put a roof over their heads? Joe, importantly, what are you going to do to end the absurdity of billionaires buying elections and the three wealthiest people in America owning more wealth than the bottom half of our people?

So, let me conclude the way I began. Donald Trump must be defeated, and I will do everything in my power to make that happen. On Sunday night, in the first one-on-one debate of this campaign, the American people will have the opportunity to see which candidate is best positioned to accomplish that goal. Thank you all very much."

March 12th 2020 Bernie Sanders Speech

The crisis we face from the coronavirus is on a scale of a major war and we must act accordingly. Nobody knows what the number of fatalities may end up being or the number of people who may get ill, and we all hope that that number will be as low as possible. But we also have to face the truth and that is that the number of casualties may actually be even higher than what the Armed Forces experienced in World War II. In other words, we have a major, major crisis and we must act accordingly. Therefore, it is an absolute moral imperative that our response as a government, as a society, as a business community, and as individual citizens meet the enormity of this crisis. As people stay or work from home and are directed to quarantine, it will be easy for us to feel like we are all alone. "I'm working at home. I'm not at my office." Or that we must only worry about ourselves and think that everybody else should fend for themselves. But in my view, that would be a tragic and dangerous mistake. If that ever was a time in the modern history of our country when we are all in this together, this is that moment. Now is the time for solidarity. Now is the time to come together with love and compassion for all, including the most vulnerable people in our society who will face this pandemic from a health perspective or face it from an economic perspective. If our neighbor or coworker get sick, we have the potential to become sick. If our neighbor loses his or her job, then our local community suffers and we may lose our jobs. We are in this together. If doctors and nurses and medical personnel do not have the equipment and the training and the capacity they need right now, people we know

Bernie Sanders Revolution

may unnecessarily face additional illness and even death. We are all in this together. Unfortunately, in this time of international crisis, it is clear to me, at least, that we have an administration that is largely incompetent, and whose incompetence and recklessness have threatened the lives of many, many people in our country. So today, I would like to give a brief overview of what, in my view, we must do to respond to this crisis. First and foremost, we are dealing with a national emergency and the President of the United States must understand that and declare that emergency. Next, because President Trump is unwilling and unable to lead selflessly, we must immediately convene an emergency bipartisan authority of experts to support and direct a response that is comprehensive, compassionate, and based first and foremost, on science and facts. In other words, Congress in a bipartisan manner must take responsibility for addressing this unparalleled crisis. Further, we must aggressively make certain that the public sector and the private sector are strongly cooperating with each other, and we need national and state hotlines staffed with well-trained people who have the best information available. One of the aspects of the current crisis is there are people who are asking themselves, "What all the symptoms of coronavirus? Well, I have a cold. Do I have the flu? Do I have the coronavirus? Who's going to help me? Where do I go to seek medical treatment? How do I get a test? When is that test going to be processed?" People have a lot of questions, and at the statewide and federal level, we need experts to provide the necessary information to our people. The American people deserve transparency. Something that the current administration has fought day after day to stifle. In other words, we need to know what is happening right now in our country, in our states, and in fact, all over the world. If there was ever a time for transparency and honesty and being straightforward, this is that moment. And we need that information coming from credible, respected scientific voices of which we have many in our own country and all over this world, not from politicians.

And during a crisis, we must make sure that we care for the communities most vulnerable to the health and economic pain that is coming, those in nursing homes and rehabilitation facilities. Those confined immigration detention centers, those who are currently incarcerated and in jails, and all people regardless of their immigration status. Unfortunately, as I think the American people increasingly understand, our country is at a severe disadvantage compared to every other major country on earth because we do not guarantee healthcare to all people as a right. And as we speak, some 87 million Americans are either uninsured or underinsured. And when you are uninsured or underinsured, you hesitate about getting the medical care you need because you cannot afford to get that medical care. The result is that millions of our people cannot afford to go to a doctor, let alone pay for coronavirus tests. So while we work to pass a Medicare for all single-payer system, the United States government today must make it clear that in the midst of this emergency, every one in our country, regardless of income or where they live, must be able to get all of the healthcare they need without cost. Obviously, when a vaccine or other effective treatment is developed, it must be free of charge. We cannot live in a nation where if you have the money, you get the treatment you need to survive. But if you're working class or poor, you get to the end of the line. That would be morally unacceptable. Further, we need emergency funding right now for paid family and medical leave. Anyone who is sick should be able to stay home during this emergency and receive their paycheck. What

Bernie Sanders Revolution

we do not want to see is at a time when half of our people are living paycheck to paycheck, when they need to go to work in order to take care of their family, we do not want to see people going to work who are sick and who can spread the coronavirus. We also need an immediate expansion of community health centers in this country so that every American will have access to a nearby healthcare facility. Where do I go? How do I get a test? How do I get the results of that test? We need greatly to expand our primary healthcare capabilities in this country and that includes expanding community health centers. We need to determine the status of our testing and processing for the coronavirus. The government must respond aggressively to make certain that we in fact have the latest and most effective tests available and the quickest means of processing those tests. There are other countries around the world who are doing better than we are in that regard. We should be learning from them. No one, none of the medical experts that I have talked to dispute that there is a major shortage of ICU units and ventilators that are needed to respond to this crisis. The federal government must work aggressively with the private sector to make sure that this equipment is available to hospitals and the rest of the medical community. Our current healthcare system does not have the doctors and nurses we currently need. We are understaffed. During this crisis, we need to mobilize medical residents, retired medical professionals and other medical personnel to help us deal with this crisis. We need to make sure that doctors, nurses, and medical professionals have the instructions and personal protective equipment that they need. This is not only because we care about the well-being of medical professionals, but if they go down, then our capability to respond to this crisis is significantly diminished. The pharmaceutical industry must be told in no uncertain terms that the medicines that they manufacturer for this crisis will be sold at cost. This is not the time for price gouging or profiteering. The coronavirus is already causing a global economic meltdown, which is impacting people throughout the world and in our own country, and it is especially dangerous for low income and working class families. People who today, before the crisis, are struggling economically. Instead of providing more tax breaks to the top 1% in large corporations, we need to provide economic assistance to the elderly. And I worry very much about elderly people in this country today, many of whom are isolated, many of whom do not have a lot of money. We need to worry about those who are already sick. We need to worry about working families with children, people with disabilities, the homeless, and all those who are vulnerable. We need to provide in that context,

Bernie Sanders Revolution

emergency unemployment assistance to anyone in this country who loses their job through no fault of their own. Right now, 23% of those who are eligible to receive unemployment compensation do not receive it. Under our proposal, everyone who loses a job must qualify for unemployment compensation at least 100% of their prior salary with a cap of $1,150 a week or $60,000 a year. In addition, those who depend on tips in the restaurant industry is suffering very much from the meltdown. Those who depend on tips, gig workers, domestic workers, and independent contractors must also qualify for unemployment insurance to make up for the income that they lose during this crisis. We need to make sure that the elderly, people with disabilities and families with children have access to nutritious food. That means expanding the Meals on Wheels Program. It means expanding the school lunch program and SNAP so that no one goes hungry during this crisis, and everyone who cannot leave their home can receive nutritious meals delivered directly to where they live. We need also in this economic crisis to place an immediate moratorium on evictions, on foreclosures, and on utility shutoffs so that no one loses their home during this crisis; and that everyone has access to clean water, electricity, heat and air conditioning. We need to construct emergency homeless shelters to make sure that the homeless, survivors of domestic violence and college students quarantined off campus are able to receive the shelter, the healthcare and the nutrition they need. We need to provide emergency lending to small and medium size businesses to cover payroll, new construction of manufacturing facilities and production of emergency supplies such as masks and ventilators, a very serious problem right now in the midst of this crisis. Here is the bottom line, and that bottom line is that in the midst of this

Bernie Sanders Revolution

unprecedented moment, we need to listen to the scientists, to the researchers, to the medical folks, not to politicians. We need an emergency response to the current emergency and we needed it immediately. We need more doctors and nurses in underserved areas. We need to make sure that workers who lose their jobs in this crisis receive the unemployment assistance they need. And in this moment, in this moment, we need to make sure that in the future, after this crisis is behind us, we build a healthcare system that makes sure that every person in this country is guaranteed the healthcare that they need. Thank you all very much.

Bernie Sanders Revolution

MIKAZUKI PUBLISHING HOUSE™

(U.S.P.T.O. Serial Number 85705702)

1. 25 Principles of Martial Arts
2. 25 Principles of Strategy
3. American Antifa
4. American Bookstore Directory
5. Arctic Black Gold
6. Art of War
7. Back to Gold
8. Basketball Team Play Design Book
9. Bernie Sanders Revolution
10. Boxing Coloring Book
11. California's Next Century 2.0
12. Camping Survival Handbook
13. Captain Bligh's Voyage
14. Coming to America Handbook
15. Customer Sales Organizer
16. DIY Comic Book
17. DIY Comic Book Part II
18. Economic Collapse Survival Manual
19. Find The Ideal Husband
20. Football Play Design Book
21. Freakshow Los Angeles
22. Game Creation Manual
23. George Washington's Farewell Address
24. GhostHuntTV Ghost Hunting Notebook
25. Hagakure
26. History of Aliens
27. Hollywood Talent Agency Directory

28. I Dream in Haiku
29. Internet Connected World
30. Irish Republican Army Manual of Guerrilla Warfare
31. Japan History Coloring Book
32. John Locke's 2nd Treatise on Civil Government
33. Karate 360
34. Learning Magic
35. Living the Pirate Code
36. Magic as Science and Religion
37. Magicians Coloring Book
38. Make Racists Afraid Again
39. Master Password Organizer Handbook
40. Mikazuki Jujitsu Manual
41. Mikazuki Political Science Manual
42. MMA Coloring Book
43. Mythology Coloring Book
44. Mythology Dictionary
45. Native Americana
46. Ninja Style
47. Ouija Board Enigma
48. Palloncino
49. Political Advertising Manual
50. Quotes Gone Wild
51. Rappers Rhyme Book
52. Saving America
53. Self-Examination Diary
54. Shinzen Karate
55. Shogun X the Last Immortal

56. Small Arms & Deep Pockets
57. Stories of a Street Performer
58. Storyboard Book
59. Swords & Sails
60. Tao Te Ching
61. The Adventures of Sherlock Holmes
62. The Art of Western Boxing
63. The Book of Five Rings
64. The Bribe Vibe
65. The Card Party
66. The History of Acid Tripping
67. The Man That Made the English Language
68. Tokiwa
69. T-Shirt Design Book
70. U.S. Army Anti-Guerrilla Warfare Manual
71. United Nations Charter
72. U.S. Military Boxing Manual
73. Van Carlton Detective Agency; Burgundy Diamond
74. William Shakespeare's Sonnets
75. Words of King Darius
76. World War Water

Facebook.com/MikazukiPublishingHouse

KAMBIZ MOSTOFIZADEH TITLES

1. 25 Principles of Martial Arts
2. 25 Principles of Strategy
3. American Antifa
4. American Bookstore Directory
5. Arctic Black Gold

Bernie Sanders Revolution

Facebook.com/KambizMostofizadeh